FUTURE HOME DESIGN

A HOME THAT ADAPTS TO DIFFERENT PHASES OF YOUR LIFE

Farinah Husodo

514 PUBLISHING
KNOWLEGE BUILDS OTHERS

© Farinah Husodo, Australia, 2021, Second edition

Published by 514 Publishing

514publishing@gmail.com

Future Home Design: A home that adapts to different phases of your life

All rights reserved. No part of this publication may be reproduced, distributed or transmitted in any form or by any means, including photocopying, recording, or other electronic or mechanical methods, without the prior written permission of the publisher, except in the case of brief quotations embodied in critical reviews and certain other noncommercial uses permitted by copyright law.

Although the author and publisher have made every effort to ensure that the information in this book was correct at press time, the author and publisher do not assume and hereby disclaim any liability to any party for any loss, damage, or disruption caused by errors or omissions, whether such errors or omissions result from negligence, accident, or any other cause.

Individuals and entities used in case studies are fictional or recreated. To the extent that some case studies may be based on actual events or situations, details have been altered to de-identify the persons and properties involved. Many of the events or scenarios described are not unique to any one person and likely describe any number of actual similar events or scenarios.

This book and its author are not affiliated with or endorsed by the State of Victoria and the Victorian Department of Environment, Land, Water and Planning. The term 'Future Home' is used in this book in a descriptive manner to refer to a home of the future. It is not connected with the 'FUTURE HOMES' Australian trade marks owned by the State of Victoria or any goods or services supplied by the State of Victoria or its licensees under or in relation to those trade marks.

The recommendations, views and opinions expressed in this book are, unless otherwise attributed, personal to the author. They are general in nature and do not constitute professional advice. If you intend to rely on any material contained in this book, you should first seek advice from an appropriate professional such as an architect or other building professionals.

Cover Design by Marko Polic (https://99designs.com.au/profiles/tintodeverano)

Interior Design by Julie Karen Hodgins

ISBN Paperback: 978-0-6451894-4-5

ISBN eBook: 978-0-6451894-1-4

ISBN Hardcover: 978-0-6451894-2-1

I dedicate this book to homeowners in Australia and all over the world. You deserve to have a place to call home—a Future Home, a home that meets your current and future needs, a home that adapts to the different phases of your life. Everyone deserves a comfortable home to raise their family, a place to build memories, and a legacy to leave for future generations.

Thank you for giving me the opportunity to guide you on the journey of building your Future Home. There is no better time to create your aspirations and dreams than now—now is the time, and this is the opportune moment.

I trust this book will empower and direct you to make the right decisions in building your Future Home.

Opportunities are like sunrises.
If you wait too long, you miss them.

WILLIAM ARTHUR WARD

BONUS SECTION

MY FREE GIFT TO YOU!

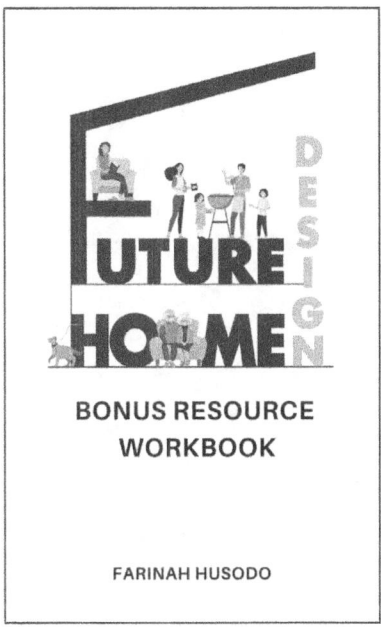

Digital Bonus Resource Workbook which includes:
- Homeowner Budget Planning template
- Long-Term Planning Chart template
- Must-Have Room List template
- Wishlist Room List template
- Other goodies!

TO DOWNLOAD, GO TO:
studiom514.com.au/bonus

CONTENTS

Chapter One: Why This Book? — 9

Section One: **FUTURE HOME** — 21

Chapter Two: What Is Future Home? — 23
Chapter Three: Future Home Features: SMALL — 29
Chapter Four: S Is for Smart — 33
Chapter Five: M Is for Millennial — 41
Chapter Six: A Is for Adaptable — 67
Chapter Seven: L Is for Livable — 89
Chapter Eight: L Is for Low Energy Consumption — 97

Section Two: **INDUSTRY SECRETS** — 117

Chapter Nine: Energy Rating — 119
Chapter Ten: Air Leakage — 123
Chapter Eleven: Overcapitalising — 129

Section Three: **MOVING FORWARD** — 147

Chapter Twelve: Increasing Trust in the Industry — 149
Chapter Thirteen: Do I Need an Architect to Build a House? — 155
Chapter Fourteen: Industry Change — 175

About the Author—Farinah Husodo — 183
Acknowledgments — 187
References — 191

CHAPTER

WHY THIS BOOK?

What is your dream home? What kind of home would you like to live in?

To some people, a home is a shelter from the weather outside. To others, a home is a memory of events, people, emotions, and feelings—a sense of place and identity.

A home can mean different things to each individual depending on their upbringing, cultural background, and society.

HOW IT ALL STARTED

In 2005 I went to Aceh, a province in the north of Sumatra, Indonesia. A devastating earthquake and tsunami that killed over 230,000 people had struck Aceh a few months earlier, on 26 December 2004—Boxing Day.

In 2005–6, after the tsunami, many organisations around the world responded by sending relief teams and volunteers to help. At that time, I was living and working in Singapore. I was part of a charitable society's volunteer team from Singapore working in partnership with one of the Indonesian non-governmental organisations (NGOs) and Habitat for Humanity for the rehabilitation and reconstruction of Aceh after the tsunami. The programme gifted each Acehnese family in the area affected by the tsunami with a 36-square-metre concrete house.

I remember the handover ceremony for the new houses, which happened during one of my trips to the island, vividly.

> **To the Acehnese, home means the people they love, the family dynamic, the powerful bond of community, and a sense of place.**

After the official handover ceremony was complete, I joined the team to walk around the grounds and chatted with the local recipients of the new houses. We asked the new owners how they felt about their new homes. I sensed from their voices and facial expressions that they were grateful. However, something else struck me about the responses; they said, 'It is not the same as my old home'.

To the Acehnese, home means the people they love, the family dynamic, the powerful bond of community, and a sense of place. The tsunami had displaced them for about one year. They were away from the neighbourhood they were familiar with; they had lost their loved ones. As wonderful as those new houses were, they were not the same as their old homes.

Those words and the look on those people's faces continue to remind me of the importance and meaning of a home. Home is a vital need for every human, and not just as a shelter or a building to protect us from the weather. It is also a collection of meanings where we keep our memories and build our history, lives, and legacy.

WHAT IS THE MEANING OF A HOME TO YOU? WHAT IS YOUR DREAM HOME?

One thing that remains the same all over the world: a home is at the heart of everyone's deepest longing and desire.

This book was born out of listening to the stories surrounding that memorable event in Aceh, Indonesia, and the stories of many homeowners back in Australia. They desired to build their dream home or renovate their current home, but were faced with many uncertainties.

> **One thing that remains the same all over the world: a home is at the heart of everyone's deepest longing and desire.**

The questions they faced are the questions you may have been asking when you picked up this book:

1. What kind of home should I build to meet my unique family needs and future life changes?
2. Where do I begin? Where do I look for useful information to get me started?
3. Who should I talk to first: a builder, an architect, a draftsperson, a building designer, or friends who have built their homes?
4. When is the right time to build? My children are growing up and soon to be young adults. Is it too late to build, when they might leave home in a few years?
5. How much do I need to invest in this building project? Is it worth it? How do I avoid overcapitalising on my project?

Listening to these questions as an architect, I found myself frustrated that even with all my training, I couldn't find all the answers. These questions led me to search for the right solutions to homeowners' needs, allowing them to have a place they can call home.

Here are some stories I heard from homeowners back in Australia.

Story One: Ian and Christina

Ian and Christina are a family with two young children, aged three and six, who live in a typical middle-class suburban house.

> 'It's an old house built in the 70s. The house gets so cold in winter that we have to turn on the heater all the time to keep ourselves warm. Once it is on for a period, it will get so hot that we need to turn it off. Once it is off, it doesn't take long for the house to become cold again. The same thing happens in summer with the air conditioning. Our energy bill skyrocketed during those chilly winter and scorching summer months.'

Story Two: Mark and Megan

Mark and Megan are a musical family with three growing teenage children aged 14, 16, and 18. The two older boys formed a pop band with two of their schoolmates.

> 'Our kids are growing up, and they've been complaining that they need more space. They want to invite their friends to hang out in the house and have privacy with their friends.'

Story Three: James and Anna

James and Anna are a family whose two children are young adults, aged 18 and 20, pursuing their higher education while living at home.

> 'Our kids prefer to stay at home to save on rental costs. They have their own rooms for privacy and a conducive environment to do their studying. They are at that independent age where home is a place for them to return to sleep and rest. Most of the time, they'll be out and about with their friends.'

> 'We enjoy our own freedom, now that they're more independent. Having them close to us gives us the comfort that they are safe and they have a home to come back to. Also, we are contributing to their future by

helping them save on rental. It goes a long way towards their tertiary fees and other education expenses.'

'However, as parents, we're constantly thinking and worried about their future in homeownership, considering the high cost of the current rental and property market. We want to help them by rebuilding this old house so they have a place to call home if they can't get into the property market. We want to leave them a legacy—a home for them to live in safely and comfortably.'

Story Four: Sam and Margaret

Sam and Margaret have two children, aged eight and ten. Margaret's parents are in their late 60s and retired, but lead an active lifestyle.

'My parents are getting old, but they've been living independently all these years. Recently, they've been doing a lot of travelling, and they get lonely when they come back to an empty house with unoccupied extra bedrooms. It also gets too strenuous for my mum to keep up with the cleaning of the house. We think it would be great if we could share a house and live together. They will enjoy the interaction with their grandchildren. The kids would love to play with Grandpa and Grandma after school or during school holidays.'

Story Five: Nigel and Doreen

Nigel and Doreen are an elderly couple in their 70s with an active lifestyle. They have been living in their two-storey family home for almost 30 years.

'We plan to sell our family home and downsize to a smaller place where we can grow old. We don't want to live in an apartment after hearing those horror stories of how badly built they are. We have gone to many open houses, but can't find anything that suits our needs. Most of the houses we saw in the market are two-storey houses with bedrooms on the first floor. Most of them are also too big, or the room layout and

corridors are too narrow and poky, which would not be convenient for a walker or wheelchair if we needed to use them.'

Those homeowners' stories disturbed me. Housing is a topic close to many hearts, including my own. I believe housing is one of humanity's basic needs. Everyone deserves to live in a healthy, comfortable home that they can enjoy with their family, friends… and even fellow Airbnb travellers, for those who are globetrotters.

During many late nights, questions would run through my head about why we end up building uncomfortable, unhealthy, badly planned homes. Is there a better way to do it? What is the number one blockage homeowners face when they plan to build their dream homes? What motivates homeowners to build their dream homes? And what is their number one concern?

As an architect, I have the privilege of listening to and understanding the common themes for homeowners' motivations, blockages, and concerns with building their dream homes.

In 15 years of working in the building and construction industry, I have been involved in various projects: detached houses, resorts, multi-residential developments, commercial fit-outs, education, and community projects. Most of the clients from the commercial, education, and multi-residential sectors have a concrete idea of what they would like to achieve and the goals of their projects.

However, I notice that homeowners in the residential sector have less knowledge and thus a lack of clarity. I work with homeowners who are uncertain of their direction, lack accurate information, and do not know where to get help. This lack of clarity leads them to confusion and inaction towards fulfilling their goals and dreams.

To be fair, this is not the homeowners' fault. Most books and much of the information available do not teach homeowners the benefit of building homes for long-term purposes. Instead, the information is geared towards viewing homes as commodities that homeowners can trade on an exchange.

In reality, most Australian homeowners stay in their house for 11.3 years on average nationally, according to CoreLogic's latest data from May 2019.[1] This trend is expected to continue upward, considering the rising cost of selling and buying property and the increasing cost of houses in major cities.

This book will equip homeowners with the knowledge they need to build for the long term, inform them on forecasted trends, and tell them how to benefit from that trend. This book will teach homeowners how to build homes that serve their current needs and anticipate future life changes without overcapitalising.

Most information and books about house building or renovating are DIY instructional books or coffee-table books with glossy pictures of inspirational designs.

Property investors write self-help books showing homeowners how to build and renovate for rental income or short-term, profit-driven property-flipping ventures. In the real estate world, articles are focused on appealing to the buyers' market.

No doubt, this information confuses and muddles up homeowners' thinking. The information sounds convincing and appealing. However, on closer examination, this advice can bring a conflict of interest. It doesn't benefit the majority of homeowners, who use their house as their primary long-term residence and for capital growth.

Most homeowners have heard or read these few golden rules. First, build or renovate your home to appeal to buyers. Second, don't invest in things that are not visible to buyers. Third, don't invest in anything a buyer won't pay for.

This advice sounds reasonable, doesn't it? But I will reveal the truth about this information in Section Two of the book, Industry Secrets.

My understanding of homeowners' challenges and concerns set me on a quest for solutions and answers. At that same time, I also wrestled with my own questions about my role and contribution as an architect in the 21st century.

In this new millennium, we face complex issues: the environmental impact of our homes and lifestyles, the rising cost of rental and property prices, elders' desire to grow old in the comfort of their homes, the millennial generation who stay longer with their parents, the rising number of homeless, and a lack of housing types to suit the changing fabric of the society we live in.

What can I do to help homeowners get the most out of their dream homes? What added value, insights, and knowledge can I impart as an architect to homeowners who are my clients, friends, or family members?

THE JOURNEY BEGINS

In 2018, this combination of homeowners' stories and my own frustrations and questions about my role and contribution as an architect set me on a journey.

I embarked on reading, researching, and thinking through methods and processes in our construction industry. I savoured articles, books, and podcasts on real estate and property investment to better understand the property market. I talked to people from different disciplines, taking a peek at their world and seeing what I could glean to find better solutions for homeowners' dilemmas.

As I dug deeper into housing and the related topics surrounding it, my passion for helping homeowners build future homes that meet their current needs and future life changes, while leveraging on capital growth, grew even more.

Over those two years, I slowly pieced the jigsaw puzzle together to form a bigger picture that made more sense. I collected a variety of information and created this resource so homeowners could plan differently for their dream homes. I'll share all of that with you in this book.

HOW CAN THIS BOOK HELP YOU?

If you are reading this book, chances are you are a homeowner or an aspiring homeowner. I wrote this book for you! It will give you insights and information to empower you in making the right decisions and choices when you build your dream home.

This book will give you:

- A success formula for putting together the components of your dream home that will stand the test of time
- Clarity on how you can plan to build a home that meets your current needs and future life changes, reducing the number of times you move and saving you associated moving costs
- Confidence in moving forward with your building project without over-capitalising and spending on things that don't benefit you directly as a homeowner
- Insights into the industry: misunderstood terms and methods
- Assurance that your home is future-ready for the next generation's use and market demand
- Useful templates and summaries as a bonus workbook to help you in your journey of building your dream home.

IS YOUR HOME FUTURE-READY?

At the turn of this century, nobody expected that 2020 would challenge us with the global COVID-19 pandemic. It required many businesses to send their employees home to work. Schools and universities had to reinvent their teaching methods to accommodate online learning from home. Is your home fit and ready for future events and social changes like the ones we experienced in 2020?

Now is the time to look closer at the homes we have designed and built in past decades and see them from a fresh perspective. Let us build future-ready homes!

WHO IS THIS BOOK FOR?

This book is FOR homeowners and aspiring homeowners who plan to build their homes to improve their quality of life, adapt to their life changes, and bring them long-term capital gain without overcapitalising.

This book is NOT FOR property investors and property flippers, whose goal is to maximise profit over a short period.

A SNEAK PEEK AT THIS BOOK

I divided the book into three sections:

SECTION ONE addresses the common questions many homeowners ask. What type of home should I build that will meet my current needs and expected future life changes? Is it even possible to build such a home?

The answer is yes—it is possible to build such a home! In fact, it's wise to build a home for long-term use. I call this concept **Future Home**.

We will dive deeper into what makes a house a Future Home. It's a home that is comfortable to live in, improves quality of life, and creates healthy, inspiring spaces—a home that's adaptable to your unique lifestyle and is cost-efficient to run in the long term.

SECTION TWO reveals some industry secrets. What are the misconceived, misunderstood, and misappropriated terms and methods? What are the myths and truths surrounding the terms *energy rating*, *air leakage*, and *overcapitalising*? How can homeowners leverage these insights to maximise comfort, reduce the running cost, and increase their homes' value without overcapitalising?

SECTION THREE gives you a bird's-eye view of current and future housing market trends from an architect's perspective. I will take you on a guided tour of my world, the world of building and construction. This section will transform you from homeowners to Future Home owners.

Even though some examples in this book are set in the Australian housing context and use Australian standards, most of the design principles and industry practices are applicable worldwide.

I trust this book will empower you to build for yourself, your family, and the generations after you a place you can call home.

Everyone is worthy of a place…

A peaceful place, a special place, a beautiful place…

A safe and restful place… they can call home.

Section One
FUTURE HOME

CHAPTER

WHAT IS FUTURE HOME?

In Chapter One, I shared five homeowners' stories and questions which sent me on a two-year journey searching for solutions, methods, and ways to solve the homeowners' dilemmas in their personal situations.

How can I, as an architect, help homeowners design and build dream homes that will meet the changing seasons of their lives?

Your family or life circumstances might differ from those stories. We are all unique in our own wonderful ways, and so are our needs and solutions. There is no 'one size fits all'!

In saying that, those stories are like the first few strokes of paint on a canvas. They don't show the picture in detail, but they provide a general sense of what the painting conveys.

Those stories represent typical Australian homes. They tell the stories of homeowners' challenges trying to fit their lives into the homes they currently live in or the homes available in the current market.

It's like when we try to squeeze into that tight-fitting dress or jeans that are way too small for us—we can't breathe comfortably or stand properly without snapping the zip or one of the buttons… ouch! It is uncomfortable and doesn't feel right.

As I termed it in Chapter One, **Future Home** is a home that serves the homeowners' current needs and future changing needs. A home that grows and moulds with their lives, a home to build long-term memories and legacy.

Future Home also means a home for future living. As technology advances, innovations to improve our lives will affect the way we build our homes. Societal change, socioeconomic development, population growth, and global challenges such as the COVID-19 pandemic demand new solutions and innovations to meet our needs for a future-ready home.

Future Home serves homeowners' needs, purpose, and lifestyle. It grows, adjusts, and moulds itself to fit the homeowners' dynamic life. It will never be a square peg in a round hole. It will be like gloves that perfectly fit the hands of the owner.

We build Future Home to serve homeowners' needs, purpose, and lifestyle—not homeowners trying to fit their lives into the confines of their home.

We build Future Home for future living to meet regional socioeconomic changes and global community events.

Let's revisit some of the stories from Chapter One.

Story Three: James and Anna. They have two young adult children who are pursuing their higher education and live at home. James and Anna are worried about their children's future home ownership in light of current high rental and property costs.

Story Four: Sam and Margaret. Margaret's parents are retired and in their late 60s. Margaret is concerned about her parents' well-being, living in a large family home—the loneliness and the daily home maintenance take a toll on them.

> **Future Home is a home that serves the homeowners' current needs and future changing needs. A home that grows and moulds with their lives, a home to build long-term memories and legacy.**

Story Five: Nigel and Doreen. They are a couple in their 70s, looking for a home to downsize to and grow old in. Unfortunately, they can't find a home in the market which suits their needs.

These stories are examples of many homeowners' struggles and desperations. They are not alone.

As homeowners, you are confronted with the reality that as your lives and your family's lives change over time, the homes you live in do not serve their function and purpose any more.

You feel restricted and trapped.

You've searched in the market for quite some time, hoping to find a replacement home or a dream home. However, those homes do not fit your needs or your family's lifestyle.

The homes available in the market within your budget range are of a similar condition and layout to your current home. Cosmetic changes might make it look new—fresh paint, new kitchen equipment, benchtop, or light fittings—but the design and feel of the spaces are familiar.

It is like walking through your current home; you can predict where the next room will be as you turn the corner of that corridor ... yep, everything is in the same place as your current home—with minor facelifts.

Interestingly, children notice this more than adults. Adults are so used to accepting life's curveballs that we have a 'nothing we can do about it' attitude. It makes us less observant, less curious, and less creative than children.

One of my nephews was 10 years old when he followed his parents to visit their friend's house in the countryside of Victoria, Australia. As he stepped inside, he told his mum he felt like he was in Grandma's house because the layout reminded him of Grandma's house in another part of Victoria.

Only after my nephew said that did his mum and dad realise he was right. The layout and the feel of the house were exactly the same as Grandma's house. What a discovery!

That story, as told by my sister about my nephew's observation, is a powerful reminder for me as an architect. A house must have its own unique sense of place, not a mass-produced, cookie-cutter feel.

How disappointing it will be to buy a new house and later realise that you're just trading your current home for another one that feels exactly the same.

Often when homeowners look for their dream home in the current market, they find that most of the newly built homes have smaller rooms than their existing home, and the blocks of land are smaller than their land.

This thought comes to mind: 'Do I want to trade the bigger plot of land for this smaller block of land and a newer-looking but smaller home?'

Another thought that crosses your mind is: 'Will this home serve the purpose of the next phase of my life and my family's life? Or will I need to move and go through the search for another home again in a few years' time?'

By the time you have a mental calculation of the costs—agent's fee for selling and buying, stamp duty, legal and other fees, moving costs, and the effort of moving and searching for the next home—you feel exhausted and discouraged. You'd rather not think about it, so you just do nothing!

You begin to think 'Maybe I should just put up with my current home or settle for something less than my dream home. We are not living in an ideal world.' Or as one of my clients says, 'You can't expect to live like a king!'

You are familiar with those feelings and struggles, and you have heard the same stories repeated by your friends and family as you exchange notes during a barbecue event. Perhaps you are amid those defining moments yourself?

What are you going to do? What can you do?

Over the years, these are thoughts I've heard from many homeowners:

- It's too expensive to engage an architect to design and build the dream home that will suit my family. Is it worth it to build a dream home? Isn't that overcapitalising?
- If I build the home now, soon my children will grow up. What am I going to do with the big house and the empty rooms?
- That is the reality of life; we just have to put up with living in our current home, or we move and find something close enough to our dream home in the market.
- Our only choice is to trade our current home for a smaller block and a smaller home that is newly built. Or we trade our existing home for a larger block and a home in a less developed area, further from city centres with long commutes to and from work and schools.

These conversations are prevalent now that the Australian housing market prices have gone through the roof in most major cities like Sydney and Melbourne.

It saddens me to think that homeowners believe they have to settle for those disheartening, dispirited, and distressing resolutions.

However, here's the good news: this book will cover some solutions I have researched for the past two years. I will unravel those solutions in the following few chapters. I trust these findings will shed some light and rays of hope into the hearts of many homeowners.

Before we move to the next chapter and go into the details of Future Home, let's look at its key characteristics and benefits:

- It is a well-thought-out and well-designed home for long-term use, so homeowners reduce the number of times they move, thus saving on the cost of selling and moving homes in their lifetimes.
- It fits homeowners' current needs and future life changes.
- It is for homeowners to enjoy as they stay in their homes for the long term and benefit from future capital growth.
- It is a comfortable, healthy, and inspiring home to live in, without high running costs.
- It can become the best gift and legacy that homeowners can leave for future generations. Taking care of future generations' housing needs ensures they always have a place to call home.

We will explore the specific features of Future Home in the next few chapters. As homeowners, you can decide which features you would like to invest in your dream home before embarking on your home building project.

I hope this book will spread the knowledge to more homeowners—homeowners who want to make a difference in their lives, their family's lives, and the wider community in the housing industry in Australia and throughout the world.

CHAPTER

FUTURE HOME FEATURES: SMALL

Now that you appreciate what Future Home can offer, let's talk about how to design and build it.

Future Home has **five key features**. I call these features **SMALL**, an acronym that groups them into specific categories.

SMALL stands for:

1. **S**MART
2. **M**ILLENNIAL
3. **A**DAPTABLE
4. **L**IVABLE
5. **L**OW ENERGY CONSUMPTION

The best thing about these features is they are not exorbitantly more expensive than any other features you would include in a standard home building project. They are not the bright shiny objects that caught your attention when you walked into the weekend open home inspection or the volume builder's home display.

> **SMALL stands for Smart, Millennial, Adaptable, Livable, Low energy consumption.**

Contrary to the real estate marketing advice of not spending on anything that buyers can't see, these features are sometimes hidden. However, they serve and benefit homeowners.

Go back to that image of a tight-fitting dress or jeans, but imagine this time you're wearing a tailor-made dress or full suit. The clothes fit snugly and perfectly in all the right places. You can breathe easy, stand tall, and enjoy the clothes like they're your second skin. Look at the camera and smile—perfect! We'll email you the photographs!

Let's look at SMALL and break it down in greater detail.

WHAT IS SMALL?

SMALL stands for Smart, Millennial, Adaptable, Livable, Low energy consumption.

SMALL is Future Home features that benefit homeowners without extraordinary costs. We will discuss each of those features in more detail in the following five chapters.

WHY DO WE BUILD SMALL?

I believe homeowners deserve to enjoy the home they have worked hard and paid so much for.

In Australia's current housing market—especially in the capital cities like Sydney and Melbourne, where house prices have gone through the roof—homeowners need to protect their home's value. It is paramount that their home has the long-term capability to serve their current needs and future life changes, have the potential for capital growth, and leave a legacy for future generations.

These are the benefits of including SMALL home features in your dream home:

- Achieve thermal comfort all year round without continually depending on mechanical heating and cooling.
- Provide good indoor air quality by using natural ventilation and non-toxic materials.
- Improve health and wellness by having a wonderful connection between indoor and outdoor areas.
- Create time savings and convenience through automation and technology.
- Build a long-term investment asset that increases your home's value, while staying in a comfortable home that meets your needs.
- Build a home that stands the test of time, improves your quality of life, and increases the long-term enjoyment of growing old in your home.
- Leave a legacy for future generations and ensure they have a place to live despite the tough housing market. It provides a leg-up for the next generation to gain assets sooner in their lives.
- Invest in features that benefit your lifestyle, health, and comfort at low running costs without extra construction costs.
- Save on the costs of moving and selling homes over a lifetime, such as agent's fees for selling and buying, plus taxes and the other costs of moving.
- Prepare for the housing market's future direction, which demands an energy-efficient home, environmentally friendly materials, and better use of land.

SMALL is Future Home features that benefit homeowners without extraordinary costs.

HOW DO WE BUILD SMALL?

- We plan and analyse carefully before starting your project.
- We have an unbiased team of experts around you to advise, guide, and empower you to make the right decisions throughout your project.
- We offer thorough research to empower you in making the right decisions that meet your needs and those of your family. You are in charge of your money, your budget, and what you want to spend it on!
- We have a long-term investment strategy instead of a short-term strategy. This enables you to stay longer in your dream home, so you can enjoy your home and build your capital growth.

WHEN DO WE BUILD SMALL?

- We build SMALL any and every time you are ready to build your dream home.
- There is no better time to build than while you still have years left to enjoy the home you have worked hard for—a home that meets your family's needs and leaves a legacy for your future generations.

WHO DO WE BUILD SMALL FOR?

- We build SMALL for homeowners and aspiring homeowners who would like to enjoy living in a quality home while leveraging on capital growth as their long-term investment.

WHERE DO WE BUILD SMALL?

- We build wherever you would like to live in your dream home.
- We can easily adapt Future Home's features to any home in Australia—in fact, anywhere around the world.

In the next five chapters, let's have a closer look at the five features of Future Home—SMALL—and their descriptions, applications, and benefits.

CHAPTER

S IS FOR SMART

In the previous chapter, we explored the Future Home features, categorised into the acronym SMALL (Smart, Millennial, Adaptable, Livable, Low energy consumption).

The first SMALL feature of Future Home is S for Smart

1. **S**MART
2. **M**ILLENNIAL
3. **A**DAPTABLE
4. **L**IVABLE
5. **L**OW ENERGY CONSUMPTION

Smart represents technology—an integrated system of technology incorporated into the home's functions.

We live in an era where technology advances rapidly to meet the needs of our fast-paced living and working environments. We are time-poor people.

Time has become a modern-day rare commodity we can't replace or get back. The best we can do is shorten the time it takes us to do things.

It's the same with our homes and the way we live our lives.

Let's have a look at one of the stories from Chapter One (Story Four): Sam and Margaret. They have two children, Chloe and Ryan, aged eight and ten.

This is one of the regular morning scenes in Sam and Margaret's household.

> 'Hey kids, we're running late! Are you guys ready with your school bags and lunch?'
>
> 'I am going to be late for work if we don't leave in the next five minutes!'
>
> Margaret, holding her car key, heads towards the garage and the car. Ryan, her ten-year-old, is behind her, ready to jump into the back seat. Chloe is still fiddling with her hair.
>
> Margaret does her usual round of checking before walking out of the house—turn off the heater and the lights, close the windows and doors, check, check, check. All good!
>
> 'Here we are,' sighs Margaret. 'Miss Chloe, are you ready? Let's get moving, please! Mummy will be late if you don't get in the car right now!'
>
> Five minutes later, the kids are finally buckled up in the back seat.
>
> Halfway down the driveway, Margaret has a sudden thought. *Have I locked the front door? I opened it to check the mailbox while I was*

Smart represents technology—an integrated system of technology incorporated into the home's functions.

waiting for the kids … arrgghh! Turning off the engine, she leaps towards the front door to check the lock. 'Oh, great, it's not locked! Where's the house key?'

Walking back as fast as she can towards the car, Margaret grabs the key from her handbag on the front seat. She slams the car door and runs back to lock the front door. Done! Now she's definitely going to be late for work. Cold sweat runs down her brow; her heart pounds uncontrollably. Walking furiously back to the car, Margaret can just imagine all her colleagues staring at her back as she walks into the office—late again!

Homeowners with young children, like Margaret, understand the frustration of going through the morning rush with incidents like this. Imagine how much time we can give back to Margaret by not making her go back to the front door to check the lock or worry about whether she missed something on one of her routine checklists.

We can incorporate an integrated smart system to different parts of your home if you are in a busy household like Margaret and Sam's.

Integrated smart systems also benefit people like Margaret's parents, who love to travel and spend a lot of time away from home. Remote operation of the integrated security alarm and lock system eases the burden of going through their home security checklist—door locks, window locks, alarm—every time they are away. The integrated lighting helps to turn the lights on and off at certain times of the day to detract suspicion from unwanted onlookers while the house is vacant during their travels.

Some applications for smart features are:

- Integrated security and locking system
- Integrated lighting system
- Integrated heating and cooling system
- Integrated sound and entertainment system.

Integrated smart features allow automation, programming, and remote operation, which benefits different homeowners' situations and needs. As technology progresses, those systems are not as expensive as they used to be. They are easy to install and user friendly.

The benefits of installing smart features in your home include convenience, peace of mind, safety, and a better quality of life. They save you time and allow you to enjoy your lifestyle more.

INTEGRATED SECURITY AND LOCKING SYSTEM

Integrated security and locking systems are becoming more common in our homes.

Some examples are:

- Keyless locking systems that operate at the touch of a button
- Remotely operated security cameras
- Combinations of a keyless locking system and security cameras.

Here are some applications where homeowners can benefit from these technologies.

APPLICATION 1: Margaret and Sam's household during the morning rush.

Locking the house with just one click eases the burden and pressure of time—this is an excellent solution for busy, time-deficient homeowners.

APPLICATION 2: Margaret's parents, going on their travels.

Now frequent travellers can have peace of mind. They don't need to worry that they missed locking one of the doors or forgot to turn on the home alarm system. Remote operation at the touch of a button covers all the bases.

APPLICATION 3: Helping out family members. Margaret and Sam's home is available when they need to let her parents in to pick up something while they are at work.

Some applications for smart features are:

- INTEGRATED SECURITY AND LOCKING SYSTEM
- INTEGRATED LIGHTING SYSTEM
- INTEGRATED HEATING AND COOLING SYSTEM
- INTEGRATED SOUND AND ENTERTAINMENT SYSTEM.

Integrated security cameras with remote operation give you complete control over who you let in when you're not at home. Not only are you able to open the door when you are not there, but you can also make sure you allow the right person in—and you can see that they leave the house with the right items you want them to take.

INTEGRATED LIGHTING

Integrated lighting provides a significant benefit to large homes, offering lots of lighting options for unique settings and moods.

It is also becoming common to use integrated lighting for security and safety purposes in livable homes. We will look at livable home features in more detail in Chapter Seven.

Some examples of integrated lighting systems are:

- Preset or pre-programmed lighting system
- Sensor lighting system.

Let's have a look at some applications and benefits of integrated lighting.

Preset or pre-programmed lighting creates a distinct mood and atmosphere for the different rooms in the house, at the touch of a button. Homeowners save time setting up the lighting every time they use the room for the same function. Preset and pre-programmed lighting can also be an integral part of your home security. You can preset some features of your home's lighting to turn on at a specific time while you are away to create the impression that someone is at home, to deter intruders.

Sensor lighting is great for outdoor security around your home. The light will turn on as it detects movement, lighting up the area where someone may be walking. Other excellent applications for this kind of movement detection lighting are for the elderly, small children, and visually impaired persons. When they need to go to the toilet at night, it illuminates the way.

INTEGRATED SOUND & ENTERTAINMENT

Homeowners who are hospitable and love to entertain their friends in their homes appreciate this smart feature.

Integrated sound and entertainment systems add value for families who enjoy a movie night on weekends, or couples who fancy a date night after the children are in bed. Imagine that the touch of a button turns on a built-in surround sound system in one of the living rooms and sets the lights to create a cinema atmosphere—all you need to add is a comfortable recliner, a glass of wine, some nuts and a bowl of popcorn. You'll have pure luxury in your own home.

Some applications of an integrated sound and entertainment system are:

- Combining your Alexa or Google voice assistant with the sound system throughout the house
- Grouping your sound system in different rooms from one command centre
- Remote Wi-Fi control or hard-wired integration of your music and entertainment equipment.

The integration combinations are endless and up to your imagination. This technology is available and ripe for those who love to indulge in music and entertainment.

The practical benefits of this system are:

- Enabling communication from one room to another within a large multi-storey or multi-level home
- For a family with young children, providing sound monitoring in the children's rooms while their parents are in another part of the home.

INTEGRATED HEATING AND COOLING

We can all appreciate living in a home with comfortable and consistent temperatures throughout.

One of the critical features for heating and cooling is the integration of a thermostat and timer. The thermostat will set the right temperature, and the timer will turn it on and off at the times you want. This integration allows you to wake up to a warm room without getting out of bed to turn it on—what a wonderful feature to have on cold winter mornings!

This integration saves homeowners the cost of running their heating and cooling systems over time. No more heating overrun or leaving home without turning off the heater.

Integrating the heating and cooling system enables you to create zones in your home. Unlike central heating and cooling, which allows only limited control over individual room settings, this feature allows personalised setting to heat or cool parts of the house that you select, ultimately reducing your energy bill and energy usage.

Integrated heating and cooling allows controlled temperature settings for comfort, health, and effective energy use for different parts of the house. It is a wise use of energy to help the planet.

You might not invest in all the Smart features. However, when you are aware of the benefits and applications of each feature, you can make the right choices that suit your family's needs.

In the next chapter, we will look at the second feature of SMALL: Millennial. We will share new inspirations that you can quickly adapt to your dream home.

CHAPTER

M IS FOR MILLENNIAL

In the previous chapter, we discussed the first feature of Future Home, Smart—an integrated system of technology incorporated into our home's functions. In this chapter, we'll look at what 'M for Millennial' means.

The second SMALL feature of Future Home is M for Millennial

1. S<small>MART</small>
2. **M<small>ILLENNIAL</small>**
3. A<small>DAPTABLE</small>
4. L<small>IVABLE</small>
5. L<small>OW ENERGY CONSUMPTION</small>

Millennial represents future living.

When viewing current world events, we see constant changes in our society, economy, family dynamics, and population.

How have those changes affected the way we design and build our homes? Do the homes we live in meet the needs of homeowners facing such constant changes?

As individuals and families, we are part of both the local community and the global village. As technology and communication advances, the world is getting smaller in terms of our connectivity with each other. But it does not isolate our families and the way we live from what is happening around the world.

As I write this book, we are still amid the global COVID-19 pandemic. Around the world, the new reality of being locked down in the confines of our home confronts all of us, and it causes an adverse impact on some of us. We have begun to recognise that our built environment can affect our emotional and mental well-being.

This pandemic has taught us to reinvent how we work and run businesses. It has even taught us to conduct online schools from home. It is high time we realised how important our homes are! They are a place of refuge, stability, and shelter amid uncertainty and confusion.

However, many homes were not designed, equipped, or ready for this global pandemic event. Many homes do not provide an environment that is comfortable, healthy, inspiring, or pleasant to stay in for months during a lockdown. And many homeowners felt stuck, closed in, and confined to a space inside their uncomfortable, dreary, lifeless and uninspiring homes.

This global pandemic is a wake-up call to most of us in the housing and construction industry. We need to change the way we design and build our homes to be future ready.

Home is where we spend most of our time outside our workplace. It is a sanctuary and a resting place after a long, busy day at work. It is the place where we raise our little ones. They crawl on the floor, touching, licking,

Millennial represents future living.

and tasting anything they can put their hands on to explore their newly discovered world.

Home needs to be a safe, healthy, and comfortable haven for homeowners. And it needs to be future-proof, so that we can deal with whatever life throws at us.

WHAT ARE THE ELEMENTS OF MILLENNIAL HOME FEATURES?

Millennial home features adapt to future living, responding to the 21st-century homeowner's challenges as our society, economy, and family dynamics change.

There are three essential elements of Millennial home features, all of which are important to future living. These are the elements that help us future-proof our homes:

1. **NATURAL MATERIALS**—the materials we use to build our home
2. **COMPACT-FOOTPRINT**—the total area we use to build our home
3. **INDOOR/OUTDOOR SPACE**—the connection between the indoor and outdoor areas of our home.

NATURAL MATERIALS

The first element of Millennial home features is natural materials.

We are increasingly conscious of eating and living healthily. We scrutinise the lists of ingredients on the food we buy from our local supermarket. More people are willing to pay extra for natural and organic food to avoid additives, preservatives, and other harmful chemicals in our food and our body.

A natural lifestyle is not limited to the choice of what food we eat. As we become more aware of the side effects of harmful chemicals, the availability of natural products has influenced other areas of our lives, too. They range from personal care products—skincare, body care, and cosmetics—to household cleaning products.

Do we make the same wise choices when we design and build our homes or select the materials we use inside them? We spend, on average, 16 hours a day inside our homes. If we live to 85 years old, we will spend 56 years and eight months inside our home. That's a sizeable chunk of our life!

What kind of environment have we created in our home? What's the quality of the air we breathe in, eat in, and sleep in?

Research findings suggest that exposure to toxins in our environment causes asthma and allergies. Around the globe, the incidence of allergy-related diseases has steadily grown over the last few decades because of the increased chemicals and toxins in our food and the environment we live in.

As a homeowner or aspiring homeowner planning to build your dream home, you must make the right choices on the materials you use in your home—materials that are natural and non-toxic—to ensure healthy living and well-being.

We want to be intentional in creating a non-toxic, natural environment for you and your family—an environment you love, enjoy, and feel inspired to be in.

What natural materials should you use for your home?

Timber

We have used timber for centuries as a building material. Externally, we use it as cladding, decking, fencing, and to build pergolas, retaining walls for landscaping, and structural posts and beams. Internally, timber is used to make flooring, doors, windows, wall panelling, joinery, benchtops, and furniture.

Timber is an old favourite because it's such a versatile material to use in and around our home. As long as it is sourced responsibly, timber is a sustainable, environmentally friendly, natural, and renewable material. Our health and well-being are enhanced when we surround ourselves with natural materials in our home.

There are three essential elements of Millennial home features

1. NATURAL MATERIALS
2. COMPACT-FOOTPRINT
3. INDOOR/OUTDOOR SPACE

Bamboo

Fast growing and sustainable, bamboo is a very versatile material, similar to timber in its application. However, bamboo has its unique properties, including high compression strength like concrete and a high tensile strength that's comparable to steel.

Unlike timber, which takes many years to grow, bamboo is a fast growing, renewable resource and has gained attention in recent years.

We use bamboo for our homes internally to make flooring, wall panelling, and furniture. Externally, it is used in many Asian countries as a scaffolding material.

There has been growing interest and research in recent years in using bamboo as a construction material, including studies on homes built entirely from bamboo. I believe we are yet to discover the potential of bamboo as a modern building material.

Natural stones

Natural stones are classic materials that don't go out of date and are long lasting. We use natural stone such as sandstone, limestone, bluestone, and slate for external and internal walls, flooring, and landscaping. Internally, we use natural stones such as marble and travertine for flooring. We can use granite and marble for benchtops in the kitchen or bathroom, and for tabletops.

Bricks and concrete blocks

Bricks are man-made from naturally occurring materials and elements: clay, sand, water, air, and fire. No toxic substances are added in the process of making them. Brick is an inert material that doesn't react with other materials and does not release toxic substances or allergens. We often use bricks to build external walls for their non-combustible and low-maintenance properties. We also use bricks to make landscaping features like paving, garden edging, and retaining walls.

Concrete blocks are made from cement, sand, aggregates (gravel and crushed stone), and water. We can use concrete blocks to build external and internal feature walls. Externally, we use concrete blocks for landscaping, such as for retaining walls.

These are natural materials you can use for your Future Home. They are readily available in most parts of the world.

What materials should you avoid for your home?

Non-eco-friendly paint

We have large surfaces inside our homes that are made from non-natural materials—the walls and floors. Those areas carry the risk of releasing toxins that will affect the quality of the indoor air we breathe.

Non-eco-friendly paint contains volatile organic compounds (VOCs). VOCs are unstable carbon-based gases that emanate from the paint as it dries. Their presence is indicated by the sharp smell of freshly painted walls; however, some paint still releases VOCs into the air years after the painting job is complete.

The VOCs from paint often include chemicals known as carcinogens (cancer-causing substances), but they can also cause irritations, headaches, respiratory problems such as asthma and allergies, and skin sensitivity.

We use low-VOC paint, zero-VOC paint, or plant-based paint for their eco-friendliness. Another alternative is to use natural wall materials such as timber panelling, which we can leave unpainted.

Non-eco-friendly adhesive

We commonly use adhesives and glues as the fixing method for natural materials and surfaces in our home, but they can also be present in natural products such as plywood or pressed wood that use formaldehyde-based resin.

Just like paint, these adhesives are comprised of VOCs, which can trigger a range of health hazards and affect the indoor air quality of our home.

A better solution is to use environmentally friendly adhesives with low VOC levels, or to avoid using materials that include adhesives as fillers and fixing methods as much as we can.

Carpet

There are pros and cons to using carpet as a flooring material. We use carpet in our homes to give a softer feel and warmth, and we can choose carpet made from natural fibres, like wool. However, it is difficult to maintain this surface free from dust and mites. If you or any of your family members are sensitive or allergy-prone, it's better to avoid using carpet as flooring.

The fixing of carpet onto the floor substrate also requires adhesives—which, as discussed above, contain VOCs and pose a risk to your family's health. Overall, carpet has been falling out of favour as a flooring material for most modern homes.

COMPACT-FOOTPRINT: THE TOTAL AREA WE USE TO BUILD OUR HOME

The second element of Millennial home features is their compact footprint.

What is a Compact-Footprint home?

The essence of a Compact-Footprint home is that **'less is more'**.

There is no specific definition of the size of a Compact-Footprint home; we create a Compact-Footprint home by maximising the floor plan layout. One simple way to do this is by reducing the number of rooms and the room sizes.

There is a significant benefit in reviewing the function of each room in your home. Ask yourself questions like:

- What are the rooms you and your family use every day?
- What is a good size for each room?

- What do you want the room to feel like?
- How often do you use it?

Make a list of the rooms you need and the size and function of each one. That will be your 'Must-Have Room List'.

Then you can make another list called 'Wishlist Room List' for the additional rooms you might like to have. This list includes the same information (size and function of each room) as your Must-Have Room List. It is a good idea to consider carefully before adding that extra room you think you need. It will surprise you how many rooms you can reduce by doing this simple exercise.

I recommend that homeowners have both room lists before starting their home design process. Those room lists will be a handy guide when you're working with the architect. They will form part of your design brief.

You can download and print the templates of the Must-Have Room List and Wishlist Room List from the Bonus section of this book.

A bigger home doesn't always mean a better one. In the same way, having a Compact-Footprint home doesn't mean you will feel cramped. You don't have to compromise on the quality of space even when you adopt a Compact-Footprint home. In fact, you will get better value for your money by having a quality space you love and enjoy being in!

Australia is among the countries in the world that build large homes. The average new free-standing home built in Australia in the 2018–9 financial year covered an area of 228.8 square metres, according to data from the CommSec Home Size Trend Report[2]— although according to the same report, this average size had dropped since the peak of 248 square metres in 2008–9. In terms of its house sizes, Australia is just behind the United States, which tops the world with an average new home area of 240.4 square metres in 2018 as stated from the same report.

The size of your home matters!

Why do I say that? Two major factors make your home size matter. These factors influence the cost of building homes in major cities in Australia and around the world; they are land cost and construction cost.

1. The cost of land

Land is a non-renewable resource and limited in supply. Therefore, as the population increases, the demand for land increases, and land prices climb.

Larger plots of land also disappear because of subdivision to meet housing demand in most major cities. Land parcels, especially in the more developed areas with better infrastructure and access to city centres, are smaller.

Real estate has peaked in many Australian cities over the last few decades. The average capital growth of property in hot spots or growth suburbs in major Australian cities like Sydney and Melbourne is around 6–7.2% a year, or a doubling in value every 10–12 years for the past decade.

Every homeowner and aspiring homeowner needs to be aware of this reality. It's important to understand this cause and effect so you can maximise the use of your land. A wise homeowner would ride on this principle when planning to build their Future Home.

Future Home allows you to leverage the capital growth of the land to increase your home's value while enjoying the benefit of living in your dream home.

2. The cost of construction

The cost of materials and labour affects the construction cost of a home, which historically has increased every year in major cities in Australia. According to Rider Levett Bucknall (RLB), 2019 (before the COVID-19 pandemic) saw increases in construction costs of 3% in Melbourne and 4.1% in Sydney.[3]

> **Two major factors make your home size matter.**
> 1. THE COST OF LAND
> 2. THE COST OF CONSTRUCTION

How would you, as a homeowner, change your strategy in building your dream home to keep up with the rising cost of land and construction? From my two years of research, Compact-Footprint is one of the promising solutions to overcome those challenges.

Benefits of a Compact-Footprint home

What are the benefits of building a Compact-Footprint home?

- **SAVINGS ON CONSTRUCTION COSTS**—A compact home means a smaller footprint, which translates to fewer materials used to build your home and more savings in construction costs.
- **BETTER-QUALITY HOMES**—The savings from the cost of material and labour in Compact-Footprint allow homeowners to spend their money to build a better-quality space and use better-quality materials for their home—spending where it counts.
- **INCREASED RESALE VALUE**—A Compact-Footprint home requires a well-considered design to maximise limited space. Good design means a well-thought-out layout that eliminates wasted space, provides good natural lighting, and creates a well-functioning space. Those are valuable features that appeal to homeowners and homebuyers. Desirability means a potential increase in resale value when or if you sell your home.
- **REDUCED RUNNING COSTS**—A compact home has less area to maintain and requires less energy to heat and cool. It also means a reduction in the running costs and energy bills of your home.
- **MAXIMISED USE OF LAND**—Homeowners in urbanised cities with access to only small parcels of land would benefit by building a Compact-Footprint home, which makes the most of a small area of land.

- **ENVIRONMENTAL BENEFITS**—Compact-Footprint homes use fewer building materials, which means we produce fewer materials, use less energy, and create less waste. We help our planet by preserving its resources to last longer.
- **ENHANCED LIFESTYLE, HEALTH, AND WELL-BEING**—Compact-Footprint homes promote a less cluttered space and foster a lifestyle of enhanced health and well-being.

Characteristics of the Compact-Footprint home

The characteristics of a Compact-Footprint home are:

1. 'Less is more' design
2. Clever hidden storage to maximise space
3. Bright and airy space
4. A room with a view.

'Less is more' design

One characteristic of a Compact-Footprint home is its 'less is more' design. By adopting this design strategy, we can gain a sense of having more room—in other words, the room feels spacious—even though we have a smaller footprint.

If we pay attention to how we move and live in our current home, we soon realise that we don't use all the space in our rooms—and in fact, we hardly use some rooms at all. It is not the quantity or the size of the rooms, but their quality, that helps us feel a room is extraordinary and extra special.

The trend of 'keeping up with the Joneses' is not what we are trying to follow in our design. We are not building bigger for a better home. We are building less area to achieve more. Think of the 80/20 rule: 80% quality with 20% size.

How do we achieve 'less is more' design?

We can achieve this design by applying the following two principles:

1. Streamline the number of rooms

In Australia, we describe a house configuration with the number of bedrooms, bathrooms, toilets, and garage. Other rooms—the living room, kitchen/meals area, laundry, and family room—are the standard rooms that come with almost every house design.

I worked and lived in Singapore for several years after I graduated from the school of architecture. Over 90% of Singapore's population live in apartments as their home, so I learned to appreciate compact design when I stayed there.

Singaporeans describe their apartments' configuration by the number of rooms instead of the number of bedrooms. The typical apartment configurations are the three-room flat, four-room flat, and five-room flat.

For example, a three-room flat has one living/dining area and two bedrooms. A four-room flat comprises one living/dining area and three bedrooms. Here is where it gets confusing: a five-room flat is not one living/dining area and four bedrooms. A five-room flat has the same configuration as a four-room flat, but with a bigger total area. Other variations are available; however, those are the main basic configurations.

In recent years, Singapore's public housing department, the Housing and Development Board (HDB), introduced a new configuration called 3Gen flat.[4] This is a multigenerational flat catering to elderly parents who live together with their married adult children's family. The design allows four bedrooms, two of which have en suite bathrooms. It is the only government flat with a four-bedroom configuration, while all the other configurations have a maximum of three bedrooms.

As you can see above, Singapore's home apartments have a very streamlined configuration compared with most homes in Australia and the United

States. The floor area is also very modest, ranging from 54 square metres for a three-room flat to 115 square metres for a 3Gen flat.[4]

Living in Singapore taught me the importance of maximising the function of every room in a home. Most rooms can be multifunctional and multipurpose. A living room can double as a family room where the family gathers or watches TV; the dining area and dining table can turn into a study area.

Living in a compact home may foster stronger family bonds if we give careful thought to design considerations for every space.

In Australia and the United States, we build houses bigger than any other country. We can adopt a Compact-Footprint design by adjusting the way we build our home.

Many homes have a formal dining room—which is rarely, if ever, used. Most families will use the meals area for everyday living activity, instead of a formal dining room. Even when we entertain, rarely do we sit around in a formal dining area. In this 21st-century lifestyle, the kitchen is the hub and the heart of most homes.

We can extend the use of the kitchen and meals area to include a family area and study corner. This arrangement might suit a family with young children. Mum and Dad can prepare meals in the kitchen while also supervising the young ones.

There are many ways for you to innovate in your home to make it more comfortable, usable, and fit for your unique purpose and lifestyle. There is no limit to what you can do to make it your unique Future Home. It is a home you will enjoy for many years—your prized possession. You deserve to enjoy and design it just the way to suit your lifestyle.

Here is another example of how to innovate the use of the rooms in your home. Instead of a formal dining room, you might like to opt for a more spacious kitchen and meals area. You could purposely make this space more spacious to entertain your guests, extending it to indoor/outdoor space to create that sense of spaciousness by visual connection. We will discuss indoor/outdoor space flow in more detail in the next section.

2. Think of quality, not quantity

We achieve 'less is more design' by thinking of quality and not quantity.

A corner of a house that catches the sunlight at different times of the day and in different seasons can be a perfect spot to sit, meditate, or daydream. Perhaps you can enjoy the warmth of the sun in winter in that one spot.

One Singapore apartment I stayed in had a bedroom window that caught the perfect sunrise. One morning, I woke up when the dawn lit the sky with its beautiful pinkish, pale orange, and yellow light. It was so memorable that I can still remember how it felt until this day. The bedroom size might have been modest, but the position of the window made that room rather special.

Creating a space with character, meaning, and memory in your home doesn't require an enormous area. It just requires your imagination, a sense of beauty, and a personal touch.

After working for many years as an architect, I've found everyone has a unique sense of beauty. Our upbringing, culture, and life experiences can influence that sense—it becomes as personal and individual as our colour preferences.

The sense of space, how you feel about the room, and how the room makes you feel are the qualities you can bring to every room in your home. There is no extra cost to make those rooms as inspiring and memorable as you can imagine them to be—they are yours to explore, yours to express in your own style.

You can do another simple exercise to add to your Must-Have Room List and Wishlist Room List. Add a column next to your list of rooms and label it 'Character of the Room'. Describe how you want each room to feel. Put in as many details as you like. That will be a helpful design brief when you work with your architect to design your Future Home.

The template is available for you to download and print from the Bonus section.

Clever hidden storage to maximise space

Another characteristic of a Compact-Footprint home is the use of hidden storage to maximise limited space—clever, organised, well-concealed storage is like a hidden treasure.

Designing Compact-Footprint homes doesn't mean we do away with storage. We might adopt the minimalist lifestyle, but we still have possessions to store. Including clever hidden storage in our plan will create a clean-cut, less cluttered space which gives the illusion and feeling of spaciousness.

Ideas for cleverly hidden storage include:

- **LAUNDRY CUPBOARD**—A cupboard can be a piece of free-standing furniture or built into the wall. Some cupboards have shelving; some are just empty space, depending on their use. Either way, it is concealed storage space behind doors. Instead of having a separate laundry room, you might consider a laundry cupboard to save space. You can house the washing machine and dryer inside the cupboard, neatly hiding these unsightly items behind the cupboard doors once you have done your activity.

- **PANTRY/BREAKFAST STATION CUPBOARD**—Do you wish you could free up space on the kitchen bench from the toaster or coffee percolator? You don't want to take out and put away that equipment from the cupboard every day, yet you also want to free up the benchtop. The dual-purpose pantry and breakfast station—similar in concept to the laundry cupboard—could be the solution for you. You can have the best of both worlds! You can open the breakfast station cupboard doors, folding and tucking them into a side pocket of the cupboard walls. You will have a full view of the cupboard and prepare your breakfast. You can close it off when you finish, and voilà! The unsightly equipment disappears inside the cupboard.

- **MURPHY BED CUPBOARD**—This is a handy solution for the extra room in your home. How often do we have guests visit and stay over? The extra room doesn't have to be a permanent guest room if we can stow away the bed neatly inside the cupboard. This frees the room for other uses, such as a study room or online meeting room.
- **STUDY STATION AND LIBRARY**—This is an excellent solution when you don't have a study room, but you need a study corner to separate little Johnny from his sister while they're both doing their homework. You can carve out a multipurpose study station and library that can appear and disappear from a concealed cupboard space.
- **RAISED BED WITH DRAWER STORAGE UNDERNEATH**—We can never have enough storage space. Why don't we make use of the room underneath the bed for that extra storage?
- **STORAGE UNDER SEATING BENCH**—Maybe you are one of those people who love to sit by the window to read a wonderful book or browse through your favourite magazine. If that's you, then claim that spot by the window and build a box seat for your reading or sitting alcove. That box seat can have a dual purpose with storage space underneath it.
- **STORAGE UNDER THE STAIRCASE**—Storage in a compact home is a necessity; claiming the space under the staircase is essential but often overlooked! I recommend drawers or shelves instead of a storeroom. Drawers and shelves often remain better organised and less cluttered than a storeroom.

These custom-made, hidden storage solutions will be more expensive than the ready-made, free-standing storage you can buy at the store. However, they're a valuable feature for space saving and creating a minimalist, clean-cut look. You can offset the cost of building a large home with this custom, clever storage. The choice is yours!

Bright and airy space

The third characteristic of a Compact-Footprint home is bright and airy space.

As a homeowner, do you have a favourite space in your home? Which is the space you most love to be in? What is inspiring about that space? Those are questions and observations that will guide you as you plan to build your dream home.

You might notice that the room's size is not necessarily the reason why you love a particular room in your home. Examine what you find appealing about the room you love.

As humans, we tend to love bright and airy spaces—spaces and rooms with good natural light and ventilation. Natural light and air create movements through the room. Sunlight creates patterns on the floor as it moves throughout the day. It provides warmth and a sense of time. I liken the feel of the breeze as it passes through the room on different days and seasons of the year to a breath of life and fresh air from nature. It gives us a connection to nature and the outside world.

Through this feature, we extend our inside home to the outside world, creating a feeling that the indoor space is larger than it actually is.

Here are some ways to create a bright and airy space:

- Place windows, highlight windows, and skylights in strategic places to allow natural light and air movement. Light creates a room that feels spacious and airy.
- Add volume to a room by increasing the ceiling height. High ceilings change the feel of a room, even if it's a modest size. Increasing the height will increase the spacious feel of the room because of the increased volume.
- Adopt an open-plan layout wherever possible. This will open up the space to allow more light into the room.
- Arrange your rooms to flow smoothly and continuously from one part of the home to the other. As much as you can, avoid designs with turning corners or transition space, like internal corridors.

- Use monotone colours throughout the house, not contrasting colours. You can add a small amount of contrasting colour in feature walls or furniture to create pop-up colours for interest.
- Use a light colour for floors and walls. Dark-coloured flooring materials, especially if they contrast with your wall colour, will highlight the floor area, making the room's size more apparent. Light colours feel spacious because they bounce light. Dark colours absorb light and compress the space.
- Avoid adding elaborate trims on windows, doors, skirtings, and cornices. The simpler and more streamlined the trim, the more spacious the room will feel. If you have existing trim that needs to remain, paint it the same colour as your walls. The fewer contrasting colours used, the better.

A room with a view

The last characteristic of a Compact-Footprint home I want to discuss is 'a room with a view'.

I liken a room with a view to the way in which our eyes see the world. The view gives us a connection to the outside world and widens our perspective. Thus, no matter how small the room, a room with a view provides a sense of openness and expansion. A view does not limit the room to the floor area but stretches it as far as the eye allows.

During the COVID-19 pandemic, when working from home, you would have noticed a lot about the function of your home. What did you discover about it? Do you have a room with a view in your home? Did you get to enjoy that room as your working space?

I love my home office space, which used to be a bedroom. It is an inspiring space for me to do my work. If you ask me what makes that room inspiring, I would say that it's the feeling and sense of space.

There is nothing fancy about the size or the decoration of the room. It's a modest size, less than 11 square metres in area, and it has one longish, narrow, north-facing window that overlooks a part of the garden.

Let me take you on a tour! You might need to stretch your imagination to experience what I see and how I feel. Here we are!

On the south side of the room is the door. Next to the door is a row of shelves along a wall and a small bar fridge. Sometimes I use the top of the bar fridge as a worktop for light food preparation. This is the 'functional corner'.

The west side of the room has a built-in wardrobe and a low bookshelf. I make use of the built-in wardrobe doors as a display board for my hobby paintings. They make the perfect backdrop, because they're white.

The low bookshelf next to the built-in wardrobe holds my frequently used files and favourite books. On top of the bookshelf is my favourite dried flower arrangement in a transparent glass vase with coloured stones inside, framed certificates, and records of other achievements. That is the 'inspirational corner'.

On the north side is the long, narrow window overlooking part of the garden. It's the only view of the world outside from within this room, but the view is pleasant and the morning sun streams through the window, warming the space in the cold winter months. The window also serves as a lookout to the garden. Next to that window is a table for my creative art activities. Yes, I take breaks from architecture work from time to time! This is the 'fun and creative corner'.

The last corner of the room, on the east side, is where my architecture work desk sits. It is a long desk that holds a computer, a desk organiser, and some potted indoor plants. I love the greenery because it adds colour to the room and brings relief to my tired eyes. I call this corner the 'action corner'.

Potted indoor plants are a wonderful addition to a workspace. It's refreshing to look at living, growing things amid the workspace. Research also shows that some indoor plants are natural air purifiers. It increases health and well-being to surround ourselves with nature and natural materials in our home. You can learn more about this topic and concept by googling 'biophilia design'.

As you can see from my workspace description, there is nothing fancy about the room shape or its construction. But one simple element, the north-facing window, is a delight to my senses. It gives me an eye relief to the outside world, warmth, and a cheerful feeling from the sunlight that streams through it.

It also awakens my sense of smell when a breeze blows in the aroma of fresh-cut grass and fragrant flowers from the garden. Depending on which month or season of the year, the wind might also deliver the smell of the next-door neighbour's barbeque!

So that's what I notice and love about my home environment. What have you noticed about yours? What would you change or improve about your current home if you were to build your dream home?

As you observe your current home, think through what makes a room comfortable and special to you; with some attention, you'll discover the features that matter to you. It will give you a new perspective on what makes an excellent investment for your dream home.

Take notes of those features and keep them as part of your design brief.

The future of the Compact-Footprint home

Compact-Footprint is a Future Home feature that is easy to adopt and versatile in its application. Whether you have a large or small plot of land, a Compact-Footprint home could be the solution for your family's Future Home.

Homeowners with a limited initial budget, such as first-time homeowners, could adopt Compact-Footprint as a strategy to build their home in stages. As your financial capabilities increase over time, you can grow your home to include your extras and Wishlist Room List.

If you adopt this strategy, I recommend that you work with your architect to design a master plan. The master plan would include the current and future stages of what you plan to build. This way, whether or not you go ahead with the future stages, your home layout will work beautifully.

Having a well-thought-out plan right from the beginning avoids a haphazard or cut-and-paste look. You'll have consistency and continuity in the theme, style, and functionality. You will also save on the unknown contingency costs, which are often in the nature of a home extension and renovation project.

This is the benefit of building a Future Home. It allows adaptability and flexibility to meet the homeowners' current and future needs.

As we have mentioned, a Compact-Footprint home is especially favourable in an urban context where land is scarce and plots are small. The Compact-Footprint feature allows homeowners in urban areas to build high-quality, well-designed homes.

Whether you are a homeowner in Australia or another part of the world, Compact-Footprint is one of the most versatile features and will make your home fit for future living.

Housing diversity and housing affordability

Today's society is experiencing housing challenges globally, even in developed countries like Australia, the United States, and the United Kingdom. The two significant challenges are housing diversity and housing affordability.

Changes in the social fabric, socioeconomic factors, population growth, and family dynamics call for innovative housing for future living. These societal changes affect both current and aspiring homeowners.

Societal and demographic changes such as smaller families, a growing number of single people, and an ageing population create a demand for housing diversity. We built our current housing stock to meet the needs of larger families. We have been building two-storey, four-bedroom, two- or three-bathroom homes with double garages in our suburban housing for decades.

This big family home model doesn't serve the purpose of, and is less affordable to, the growing market of smaller family units, singles, and downsizers. The Compact-Footprint home is one of the promising solutions I see emerging in current and future markets to close this gap.

Homeowners who adopt a Compact-Footprint feature for their Future Home will benefit in two ways. They will enjoy the feature as homeowners living in it; and when or if they sell, the market will be ready for it.

Most highly populated cities around the world are also experiencing a crisis of housing affordability. It's a disconcerting phenomenon for future generations who can't access affordable housing and homeownership.

We cannot control the rising cost of land, which is one of the drivers of housing unaffordability. However, we can easily adopt the Compact-Footprint home to share the limited land resources with more people and make it affordable. Sharing is caring.

The tiny house movement

What is a tiny house? Is a tiny house the same as a Compact-Footprint home?

Tiny house is a specific term used in the industry to define the small home movement. Based on the 2018 International Residential Code, Appendix Q, the definition of a tiny house is a dwelling that is 400 square feet (37 square metres) or less in floor area, excluding lofts.[5] Even though a tiny house has a compact footprint, it is not what we define as a Compact-Footprint home in this book.

In the past few years, in Australia and other places worldwide, tiny houses have been widely publicised and have become a bit of a fad. The rising cost of housing and the challenge of housing affordability has made them an attractive alternative housing model.

A tiny house has its appeal because it is easy to build and costs less than a typical house. Many tiny houses, because they are on wheels, have the additional benefit of being transported easily. They can be attached to the car's tow bar like a caravan and parked on most land conditions with little site preparation.

In Australia, some municipalities and councils allow the construction of tiny houses with wheels, and one can park a tiny house on their land with no planning permit. However, homeowners need to check with their local council before rushing to order a tiny house from the manufacturer. Some manufacturers do not include the permit application as part of their service.

Even though a tiny house can solve the rising costs of land and construction, the restriction on the specific size—37 square metres or less—is not everyone's cup of tea. Few homeowners are prepared to downsize their dream home to a tiny house.

A Compact-Footprint home is less restrictive in the total footprint size. It is up to homeowners to determine the right size for their lifestyle. Just bear in mind that Compact-Footprint means having a smaller-than-average home. We call it compact for a purpose!

I believe Compact-Footprint goes hand in hand with the next aspect of Future Home's Millennial features: indoor/outdoor space.

INDOOR/OUTDOOR SPACE: THE CONNECTION BETWEEN INDOOR AND OUTDOOR

The third element of Future Home's Millennial features is indoor/outdoor space.

At the time of writing, we are amid the COVID-19 global pandemic; most of us are homebound. For the first time in modern history, our homes have more meaning and function than just a dwelling place. Our home's role has become broader; it's now a home, office, school, gym, boardroom, conference room, workshop, studio, and so on.

Could this be the new normal of living? We hope not! But what's interesting is the way in which we have gained valuable insight through this global event into the importance of our environment, especially our home—now the place where we spend the most time.

How can we build a home that will stand the test of time and adapt to the world's changes?

Homeowners worldwide realise the significance of having a comfortable, healthy, and conducive home—a home that connects us to the outside world, fresh air, and outdoor space. Our human senses innately crave natural environments—fresh air, greenery, natural breezes, sunlight, and the sights and smells of nature.

Indoor/outdoor space awakens our senses to the sights, smells, sounds, and touch of nature. It is certainly a highly prized feature during this lockdown season. Having access to indoor/outdoor space brings a breath of fresh air, literally, when we have to spend countless hours within the confines of our homes for seemingly indefinite months.

Indoor/outdoor space brings in natural light and ventilation to our home. And it gives us a visual connection to the outside world. Nature reduces stress and improves our emotional state and well-being.

How do we create indoor/outdoor space in our homes?

There are two ways to create indoor/outdoor space.

Extend the indoor to the outdoor

You can extend the indoor to the outdoor by designing rooms inside your home to flow seamlessly to the outdoor space, creating a blurred line between inside and outside.

A recent study in biophilia design[6] has shown that connecting humans to nature in the built environment increases health, productivity, and general well-being. Building a home surrounded by nature and connected to the natural environment creates a healthy living space that is restful and conducive to family bonding and interactions.

A living room that overlooks or opens to a courtyard or a garden claims the outdoors as part of that room. You might have a door that links directly to the garden. Or you might choose a visual connection through a full-height window. Both ways allow the room to extend to the courtyard space. Leveraging borrowed light and space is a great way to create fluidity from indoor to outdoor.

Let's use the same principle and apply it to the kitchen and meals area. We can design this area to extend to the outdoor deck—a great space for entertaining and family gatherings. If you're an avid cook, you might like the idea of extending the indoor kitchen to an outdoor barbeque kitchen area for a smoky and earthy style of cooking.

How about the master bedroom? How can we apply the indoor/outdoor principle to this space? Have you ever been to a resort and stayed in their studio bedroom unit? Did you wish you could stay there forever? Well, I might have the right place for you to do just that: your own home!

You can have a master bedroom that directly accesses a secluded part of the garden—a 'secret garden'. You can recreate your very own resort studio in your own backyard.

How do you like those ideas? Do they inspire you to build your own Future Home? How much value would developing indoor/outdoor space add to your life and your family's lives? How much more memorable would your time be if you could live in such a home?

It is simple and easy to include these indoor/outdoor designs in your Future Home, and it won't add special construction costs. Thoughtful design doesn't have to be fancy or expensive, yet it can achieve premium value when it's executed well.

Bring in the sense of outdoor to indoor

The second way to create indoor/outdoor space is to flip things around, and bring the outdoors inside.

When you have limited or no outdoor space, you can bring in the outdoor to the indoor. This approach calls for creativity and ingenuity, especially when you live in a built-up urban city—and that's where the architect's service will work to your best advantage. You need to make the most of the architect's creative and pragmatic brain!

Here are some ways to bring a sense of outdoors to the indoors:

- An internal courtyard is a great way to break up a long narrow house plan, such as a terrace house. The internal courtyard brings light and fresh air into the home. Potted plants, a pebbled garden, water features, and creeping planters along the wall are some ways to claim the internal courtyard space as your own mini-garden inside the home.
- Indoor plants in different areas of your home—where there is good lighting and air flow—are a great way to improve the indoor air quality.
- Potted herbs along the kitchen windowsill would give you a miniature herb garden. You'll have the joy of fresh herbs within your reach for your cooking. Plus, they bring in a wonderful fragrance to your kitchen.
- A vertical wall garden inside the home serves as a compact internal garden for homeowners with little or no outdoor space. The good news is that with advancements in technology, you can automate irrigation with very little fuss and mess.

I believe homeowners must be aware of how they live in and use their homes. Looking to the future, what kind of home do you want to live in? Home is the biggest— sometimes the only—asset a person has in life. We all want to enjoy, protect, and grow this asset.

In the next chapter, we will look at the third Future Home feature, Adaptable. It's a jam-packed chapter, full of ideas on how to plan for future living. Let's dig in and open the future panorama!

CHAPTER

A IS FOR ADAPTABLE

We discussed two Future Home features in previous chapters: Smart represents technology, and Millennial symbolises future living. Now let's look at the third feature.

The third SMALL feature of Future Home is A for Adaptable

1. **S**MART
2. **M**ILLENNIAL
3. **A**DAPTABLE
4. **L**IVABLE
5. **L**OW ENERGY CONSUMPTION

Adaptable represents the ability of the home to adapt to the homeowner's changing needs.

The adaptable feature is economical and achievable if planned for the long term. It is also the smart thing to do to prepare for future housing market directions. It will give homeowners the advantage of growing their asset while enjoying their home.

Long-term planning is essential in designing a Future Home with adaptable features. This third feature of SMALL will save homeowners tens of thousands of dollars on the cost of selling, buying, and moving houses over their lifetime—tax, stamp duty, agent's fees, bank fees, and so on—not to mention the stress of moving homes!

WHAT DOES LONG-TERM PLANNING LOOK LIKE?

Long-term planning follows four fundamental principles:

1. **KNOW YOUR WHY**—In his book *Start with WHY*, Simon Sinek says that our WHY is the purpose, cause, or belief that motivates us.[7] Homeowners need to dig deeper into their WHY. Why do you want to build your dream home? What is the reason or purpose that motivates you to build it? Knowing your WHY will give you the clarity to plan for your long-term goal.

2. **DETERMINE YOUR TIME FRAME**—Specify the time frame for which you plan to stay in your dream home. Some homeowners say, 'We don't know what will happen in the future, so we don't know how long we will stay in this home.' I get that; nobody knows what will happen to us in the next hour, let alone many years ahead, and we can't plan for the unknown. However, we can create a plan based on the way our lives have progressed so far. We have to start somewhere! Not knowing the future doesn't mean we can't plan our lives or aspire and dream.

   Another way to gauge the time frame is to go back to your WHY. For example, if your WHY for building your dream home is to grow old in your own home, your time frame

> **Long-term planning is essential in designing a Future Home with adaptable features.**

might be 20–30 years, depending on what phase of life you are in. If you have a young family, your WHY might be to provide your children with a place to grow until they are ready to move out, and your time frame may be 10–20 years. Knowing the time frame will help you plan well to make better decisions regarding your investments and resources. What is the return you are expecting, both financially and in terms of lifestyle improvement?

3. **PLAN FOR YOUR LIFE CHANGES**—Once you know your WHY and set your time frame, you can plan for the expected changes in your lives and your family's lives during that time frame. Let's say we use the example of growing old in the house as your WHY. At the time of planning, your children are in their teenage years, so your current need is to provide a home for the children for another seven to ten years. Your future needs or life changes are likely to occur when the children move out, and you are at a retirement phase of your life. What kind of lifestyle do you expect to have at that time?

Assuming you want to stay in your home after the children move out, how would you like your home to adapt to your retirement lifestyle? Would you be travelling most of the time? Would you be looking into the possibility of renting out part of your home to other short-term travellers? Maybe you would like to build a community with other retired friends who choose to share a house rather than staying on their own. Perhaps you have a desire to provide for homestay students in your home.

Those are examples of life changes you can expect and make allowance for when planning to build your Future Home. When you plan ahead for the different seasons of your life, you won't be caught by surprise when those changes happen. Your home is future-proof; it is designed to adapt to meet your future needs as well as your current ones. Thoughtful planning will save you a lot of stress and tens of thousands of dollars in moving expenses. There's a great saying by

Richard Cushing that sums this up well: 'Plan ahead. It wasn't raining when Noah built the Ark.'

4. **ESTABLISH YOUR LONG-TERM LEGACY**—This is for homeowners who set their goal for a time frame longer than their own lifetime. Their goal is to leave a legacy for their children and future generations. These homeowners understand that land is a limited resource that drives up housing costs. They plan to build their Future Home to leave a legacy for future generations, as in James and Anna's story in Chapter One.

You can do your Future Home planning using the Long-Term Planning Chart template downloadable in the Bonus section.

WHAT ARE THE ELEMENTS OF ADAPTABLE?

Adaptable elements include:

- Flexible and multipurpose space
- Income generation potential
- Multigenerational living.

Let's have a look at each of the Adaptable elements in greater detail.

Flexible and multipurpose space

Flexible and multipurpose space means space that is adaptable for more than one function or purpose. If we pay close attention to how we use our home, we'll discover we can use most rooms for more than one purpose.

Carefully assess the rooms you need. We are used to adding more to our Must-Have List instead of our Wishlist, but in reality, rooms such as a formal dining room, guest room, gym, home theatre, study room, and home office may not truly be required. And remember: as your Must-Have List grows, so does the footprint and the cost. As we discussed in the preceding chapter, a bigger home doesn't always mean a better one. Quality is more important than quantity for long-term use and the lifetime value of your home.

Long-term planning follows four fundamental principles:

1. KNOW YOUR WHY
2. DETERMINE YOUR TIME FRAME
3. PLAN FOR YOUR LIFE CHANGES
4. ESTABLISH YOUR LONG-TERM LEGACY.

If you can afford to build a large home without compromising the quality, it's a bonus! But all too often, homeowners compromise on the quality and longevity of their home, opting instead for a large footprint and expensive transient items such as equipment and other interior surfaces and fixtures.

Those interior items do not last as long as quality windows or well-insulated walls, roofs, and floors. The structure and bones of your home are the big-ticket items to invest in for quality and longevity. They are items that are difficult and expensive to replace when they are of inferior quality and do not perform as they should.

You can replace and update interior items in a few years. They are more disposable and flexible than your home's fundamental structure. The bones of your home work hard for you. They protect you from the weather day in, day out throughout the life of your home.

Another big-ticket item worth investing in is your home's layout—the number of rooms and the size of your rooms. They form the footprint, another aspect of your home's basic structure.

Homeowners planning to build a Future Home can streamline the rooms in their home for multipurpose use. If you pay attention to how you and your family use the space, you'll find that some activities can share the same place. Seasonal events can use the same room as daily activities.

In Chapter One, we introduced you to families with different dynamics and needs. One of those families is Mark and Megan, a musical family with three teenagers. In the following sections, we look at some ideas for flexible use of space; one of the applications below would be a perfect solution for this family.

Study and home office/guest bedroom

Having guests stay over at our home is a seasonal event, whereas using a study room and home office are daily activities. You can design the room to hide the bed inside a built-in cupboard using a Murphy bed or wall bed concept. This frees the room for use as something other than just a bedroom. Another option is to furnish it with a sofa bed, which you can use as seating for an office or study and as a bed for a guest bedroom.

A home office doesn't have to be a permanent setup. We use the home office mainly during office hours; after that, what's stopping us from using this room as a study space, a library, or a reading room?

During the COVID-19 pandemic, when we needed to work and attend classes from home, flexible and multipurpose space proved crucial for homeowners. This kind of space would be a popular addition to most homes post-COVID-19.

Businesses would re-examine the way they do business and set up their workplace. Remote office and home working arrangements could be an attractive future direction for some companies. It could mean reduced costs due to renting smaller office space.

Home offices could be a future workplace trend, encouraging a better work–life balance for families. Home offices also benefit the environment. Imagine the amount of fuel saved and the reduction in carbon emissions because of our reduced travel to and from work with our cars.

Time saving is another significant bonus associated with the home office setting. Many working parents save at least two hours a day from their travelling time. That's equivalent to saving 10 hours a week or 21 days and 16 hours a year every year of their lives.

It benefits homeowners to future-proof their homes for what could be the future trends of home design. What will future homeowners need five or 10 years from now?

Laundry and arts/craft/sewing room

Most homes have underutilised laundry rooms. Other activities, such as arts and crafts or sewing, could share this space. These activities would benefit from the use of the laundry trough and bench space. Depending on the frequency and the time allocated for your laundry chores, it is more economical to design a bigger multipurpose room for two or three activities instead of a few smaller, separate rooms. You might also like to consider stacking the washing machine and dryer inside a well-ventilated cupboard to keep the room neater and more appealing than an obvious laundry room.

Family room and home theatre/game/recreation/music/library/study room

You can use the family room for many activities that your family loves. During the week, it might be a study room or library for your family where everyone has their specific spot to do their work, study, or reading. This space arrangement is conducive to family interactions and bonding. For parents with younger children, this might be a beneficial arrangement for parental supervision of their screen time.

On the weekend, this space can have a different feel and function. You can turn it into a home theatre/game/recreation room. Or it could be the children's entertaining zone when they have their friends over, hosting slumber parties and sleepovers. It could even be an indoor campground during the winter months when it's too cold to set up an outdoor tent.

Designing a room that is flexible and multipurpose doesn't have to be boring and rigid.

For families with teenage children—like Mark and Megan, whose elder sons are into music— the family room can double up as a music room. For them, it would be worth investing in soundproofing this room and closing it off from other parts of the home.

Living room/reading room/parents' recreation room

When a home has both living and family rooms, the living room is rarely used other than for receiving guests. As the owner of a Future Home, it's important that you intend the living room for multiple uses other than just a guests' sitting room. You can design the living room to house other activities, such as a reading room or parents' recreation room.

If you have teenage children, what if you consider the living room as the parents' zone and the family room as the teenagers' zone? This way, you can prevent the noise from travelling from one area to another and create privacy for each zone.

From my experience of living in Singapore, I saw few apartments with both living and family rooms. Most living rooms serve as both. There is an advantage to making the living room bigger if we design it for multipurpose use. That way, the extra space can create different corners for separate activities without feeling too compressed.

Garage and workshop/games room

We use the garage to house our car, mainly at night and on weekdays before and after work. On weekends, you can make use of this space as workshop space or a game room, especially if your home has carport space to park the car. Clever storage space for tools and recreational equipment is a valuable addition to this multipurpose garage.

Those are examples of multipurpose use of space. There are no limitations on how many other combinations you can develop for your Future Home to suit your family's unique needs and lifestyle.

Flexibility and creativity are the genius of Future Home design. You will increase your home's resale value by having well-designed, multifunctional rooms. Future homeowners can change and use those rooms to suit their unique needs.

What are the benefits of flexible and multipurpose spaces?
- Maximise the use of seasonal rooms
- Allow for flexibility and adaptability to your life's changes without the need to make major structural changes, renovations, and extensions
- Save on the cost of building unnecessary extra rooms.

It takes creativity, thoughtfulness, and planning to come up with a beautiful and workable design. Hiring professionals, like architects, helps you develop and implement Future Home design. I'll share more on the role of architects in Chapter Thirteen.

By taking a long-range view, you will enjoy your Future Home for the long term. You will also save the cost of moving, selling, and buying multiple homes over your lifetime. Those savings would fund a Future Home project that fits your lifestyle, plus add extra money to your pocket. And who doesn't like that?

Income generation potential

The high cost of land and property in major cities in the world prevents people from pursuing home ownership. It also creates a demand for quality rental space and home-sharing, especially among the millennial generation—depending on your definition, those born between 1981 and 1996 or between 1980 and 2000.[8]

Home ownership is a growing concern among millennials. They cannot get into the home market and are forced to rent long term. And because of the resulting increase in rental demand, it is also challenging to find excellent-quality long-term rental space.

How does all that affect current homeowners? I believe opportunities exist for current homeowners to provide rental space or home-sharing to meet the increased demand. This mindset can benefit both homeowners and tenants if the homeowners put some thought and planning into their Future Home design.

Careful planning of room layout and functionality optimises the use of each room in your home. Your home can adapt to changes in your lifestyle and circumstances. Homeowners can design their homes for potential income generation without significant renovation and structural changes if they have the foresight to plan ahead.

Matt and Joni's story

Matt and Joni are in a new phase of life; they are entering their retirement age. Their adult children are all independent and have moved out of the home. The couple loves the area they currently live in, so they are not planning to move out to downsize—but they now have spare bedrooms that used to belong to the children. What are their options?

Suppose that Matt and Joni are Future Home owners. They understood the principles of Future Home. They foresaw these life changes and planned for them when they built their home. They designed the children's bedrooms to be at the other end of the home, with a shared bathroom and a small seating area—the children's compound.

Now those rooms are free, they can rent out one or both. They could rent them out to others in their age group—perhaps a one-person household who prefers to share a home. Or they could offer that space to homestay students, or use it for short-term Airbnb travellers.

In this way, Matt and Joni won't feel isolated now that their children have moved out. They will have companionship and income to help with the home expenses.

Mary's story

Mary is a single lady in her 30s, at the peak of her career life. She builds her Future Home with the income generation potential in mind. She lives on her own and wouldn't mind sharing her home with another single person with whom she is comfortable.

Mary has designed her home with a guest compound connected to the primary residence. This guest compound is a one-bedroom studio with its own compact seating area, bathroom, and toilet. She and her tenant will share the main home kitchen and laundry facilities, but the studio has its own access from the garage and the garden walkway.

This studio would be a great rental opportunity to help Mary with the mortgage payment. And in the future, she can use it for her mum if her mum needs to be looked after when she is older.

With the immense cost of land and rental units in the current economy, many opportunities are available to share our under-used spare rooms with others—those who need rental space in a comfortable home with a good environment. A spare bedroom in a private area of the house allows privacy for both homeowners and potential tenants.

A guest compound in a studio format with a compact sitting area, bedroom, and bathroom, and a separate private entrance like Mary designed, would be a desirable arrangement for either Airbnb or higher-quality rental opportunities.

The guest compound allows connection to the main house while affording privacy. It is also essential for this section to have its own heating and cooling zones to save on the energy bill when it's vacant.

As a precautionary note, homeowners need to look into the specific tenancy legislation in the country and state where they live. It's also important to work with your local architect, who will understand the local building regulations.

Once we have taken care of the regulatory side, this Future Home feature can provide a win-win situation for both homeowners and tenants.

Homeowners appreciate good tenants who look after the rental place as their own home. The same is true of tenants, who appreciate landlords who provide a quality rental space. I can speak from my own experience as a tenant when I lived in Singapore. I appreciated my landlady for providing me with the wonderful room I rented in her home.

Multigenerational living

We live in a fast-changing society and world. Economic, social, political, and environmental changes affect us as a community and a society, both locally and globally. As the world becomes more connected, the changes we experience in one country increasingly affect other parts of the world.

Some changes we see around the world are urbanisation, ageing populations, employment changes, migration, and altered family unit structures and dynamics.

Urbanisation changes the landscape of an area. It attracts people from the rural and outlying towns, who flock to the cities for job opportunities and a better lifestyle. This movement of people affects the cost of living and housing provision in major cities around the world.

The high cost of living in cities affects the fabric and structure of family units. Job opportunities and job security affect the socioeconomic fabric of our society. Coupled with an ageing population, all these factors affect family unit configurations, family dynamics, and the ways in which families live and interact with each other.

Some of the global phenomena that affect family unit configurations and household dynamics are:

- The millennial generation remaining longer at home with their parents. The high cost of living prevents many millennials from moving out of their parental homes.
- Boomerang kids[9]—children moving back to live with their parents after living independently. Housing affordability, high living costs, and lack of job permanency are the contributing factors to this phenomenon. Adult children move out of the home as they find a stable job; however, it is common that when they experience job instability, high rental costs force them to move back to their parents' home.

- Delay in starting family life in favour of pursuing higher education or career among the younger generation. Due to changes in society's outlook, the younger generation place more value on pursuing their dreams than starting a family early.
- An increase in family breakdowns has caused shrinkage in average household size.
- Increase in single-person households caused by the elderly who live alone because of a spouse's death, a single person delaying family life, or marriage breakdown.
- Longer life expectancy and sustained low fertility result in an ageing population with fewer children compared with older people in the population.

These social changes affect how families live in their homes and the dynamics of family and household size. This creates an increased need for housing variety and flexibility to accommodate those changes.

We see different options emerge, such as the granny flat, dependent person unit, or secondary dwelling unit—terms describing a one-bedroom unit in the backyard of the main house. This type of home has become popular in the last decade. It is a solution for homeowners who wish to allow their elderly parents to grow old in their own home, having some privacy yet close enough to be cared for when needed. A unit like this can also be a home for family members with special needs who are dependent on the homeowner as their carer.

There are slight differences in the regulations among the states and local councils in Australia on the use of granny flats, with Victoria's being the toughest with regard to the definition, usage, and permit requirements. In Victoria, a granny flat is defined as a dependent person's unit for elderly or disabled family members. Once the dependent person is not living in the granny flat any more, the homeowner needs to pull it down.

In New South Wales and other states, a granny flat is a secondary dwelling that can function as an independent living unit. It has restrictions on the land size and unit size, but homeowners can rent it out as a source of income.

Other countries have their own local definitions and regulations that are unique to the area. Suffice to say, a granny flat is a type of home that responds to needs arising from changes in family dynamics.

Another type of home that responds to society and family dynamic changes is the multigenerational home. This is a home where more than one generation from the same family lives under one roof. Adult children remain with their parents (two generations living together) or adult children who have their own children live with their parents (three generations living together).

In some cultures—in parts of Asia, the Middle East, Central and South America, and southern and eastern Europe—community and family take care of the elderly, and an aged care facility is the last resort when families can't care for their older relatives. In this cultural context, multigenerational living or extended family living emerges as another housing type to provide a solution for this cultural context and lifestyle.

There seems to be a trend to go back to this lifestyle, even in western countries. Statistics show an increasing trend of multigenerational living. According to the Pew Research Center Analysis in 2016, 20% of the US population live in a multigenerational household.[10] In Australia, 'one in five Australians live in a multigenerational household' according to research from the UNSW City Futures Research Centre.[11]

Given the current socioeconomic conditions, family lifestyle and values are not the only reason families worldwide adopted this model. Economic reasons also attract families to live in multigenerational homes.

It is not uncommon for migrants in a new country to start their home ownership journey by living in a multigenerational home. This provides a way to help each household and family member to save up towards their own home.

I spoke to a homeowner in Singapore who adopted a multigenerational home model for economic reasons a few years ago. This household, living in a semi-detached, three-storey house, comprises a couple with one child, elderly parents, and another couple from their extended family. Three sets of household resources and assets merge into one multigenerational family home. This family is content to live a community lifestyle where they share household chores, expenses, and care for elderly parents within one home.

Depending on your culture and family dynamics, a multigenerational home has its place, benefits, and limitations. The key is to be aware of both sides of the coin and find the right balance that works for your family. Lisa M. Cini's book *Hive: The Simple Guide to Multigenerational Living: How Our Family Makes It Work* beautifully explores multigenerational living.[12] It shares the nuances and dynamics of a four-generation family living under one roof in the United States while caring for a grandma with dementia.

A multigenerational home, where families live under one roof for the mutual benefits of sharing resources, emotional support, and family bonding, has many advantages:

- Shares the cost of building one home instead of multiple homes
- Spreads living costs such as household expenses, utilities, maintenance, furnishings, and equipment
- Distributes household chores and responsibilities to enable a lighter burden for everyone
- Fosters strong family bonds by cultivating life skills to the young and transferring family heritage knowledge from one generation to another
- Enables family members to stay connected and close to each other
- Allows the older generation to age in the home among their family and loved ones
- Supports a family with young children by capitalising on the role of grandparents in their grandchildren's lives and lending a helping hand for childcare

- Enhances the quality of life and emotional support for the elderly by having frequent interactions with family and loved ones in a community setting
- Reduces expenses and provides a healthier alternative for the elderly to age at home compared with living at an aged care facility.

But multigenerational living also has some limitations:

- Lack of privacy is a primary issue in multigenerational living; it is important to have a workable home layout and thoughtful design to overcome this hurdle.
- Isolating noise transference from one part of the home to another is a challenge that calls for a thoughtful layout and soundproofing the walls and floors at crucial locations.
- Sharing facilities such as kitchen and laundry can also be a challenge; a good schedule and mutual understanding to meet everyone's needs without jeopardising relationships is an optimal solution.
- Lack of well-designed spaces for everyone to feel connected yet remain separate and private at different times can be a problem.
- There can sometimes be a lack of consideration for different households' routines, needs, use of space, and lifestyles; for example, families with young children or teenagers and the elderly would have different requirements in a home layout.

Design considerations for multigenerational homes

There are several aspects to take into account when designing a home for multigenerational living. Some of these are discussed here.

Upstairs and downstairs living

For a family with children and grandparents living in a multigenerational home, separating the two households between different levels could provide more privacy. The elderly family members would occupy the ground floor space as their main living compound together with the shared facilities like kitchen and laundry, while the upstairs section would be reserved for the household with children.

Everything but the second kitchen

Depending on the family dynamics, a multigenerational home might need a second kitchen to maintain harmony in the house. Sometimes, the kitchen is one facility where different households have their own firm preferences for the way it's set up and how often it's used. Differences in this area can add stress and become sticky points to manoeuvre and negotiate if they're not resolved from the beginning.

In Australia, depending on your state and the local council regulations, it might not be possible to have a second kitchen. If this is the case, a kitchenette would be an excellent compromise. Another alternative is perhaps to have two separate working spaces and sinks in the kitchen.

I hope regulations in this area will catch up with changing and growing needs. However, as is often the case, regulation takes a long time to evolve and meet the market's needs.

Separation between private and public spaces

It is valuable to create a clear boundary and separation between the different households' private spaces and the shared public spaces. A door that can be closed off between the households' private spaces would provide greater separation and privacy—a two-in-one home design solution.

Private outdoor space

Although it is not a requirement for a single dwelling to have two private outdoor spaces, this would be a splendid arrangement if space permits. For an upstairs and downstairs household arrangement, there is always the option of having a ground floor garden for one household and a roof terrace or balcony for the other. The more privacy we can create for each household, the better quality of life each family has and the happier everyone will be.

Homeowners need to be engaged with a thorough design process with their architect to create a functional and successful multigenerational home that everyone loves. A walk-through with the architect on the details of how each household uses its spaces, as well as its preferences and lifestyle, will be necessary.

My experience of growing up in a multigenerational home

I grew up in a multigenerational home in Indonesia during my childhood years before our family migrated to Melbourne.

We lived in a two-storey terrace house in a dense urban area in Jakarta, the capital city. It was a narrow, deep house layout. In southeast Asia, we often use this layout as a shop-house—with a shop or office downstairs and the residence upstairs.

We used our family terrace home as residential accommodation, both upstairs and downstairs. We lived with grandparents and uncles and aunties before they got married. It was my grandparents' culture and tradition for family members to live together until they marry. However, my dad, the eldest son, remained in the family home with his own family and my grandparents.

As a child, I had mixed feelings about living in a multigenerational home. The positive part was that I never felt alone. As well as my siblings, there were always adults available to talk to, play with, and learn from while our parents were out at work. There were more interactions between generations to pass on culture, family values, and traditions.

With curiosity, I watched my grandma make her special dessert and traditional food during festive seasons. It was a labour of love for the family, her way to honour the culture and traditions she had learned from past generations. Grandma's elaborate food preparation, the variety of spices she used, and her unique way of wrapping them are fond memories.

Grandpa was a herbalist. He mixed special herb concoctions if anyone in the family was not well—they seemed to cure any sickness! I loved watching Grandpa weigh his herbs using the traditional balanced weighing scale. It took great skill to know how to balance those scales accurately and read the weight!

As a curious child, living in a multigenerational home instilled in me a sense of exploration to discover new learning. I learned early in my life that I could ask an adult to teach me or show me how to do certain things I saw them doing. For example, I learned to use Grandma's Singer sewing machine to make my doll's dress. It was a fun project!

The part I didn't quite enjoy was the cramped space and the noise. Our home was compact compared with current standard homes in Australia. As an introverted, imaginative child, I preferred to look for quiet corners in the house, away from the noise, where I could read a book, do my art and craft, and get lost in my world of thoughts.

Living in a multigenerational home taught me the concept of sharing the public spaces in the home. I understood the hierarchy of family life, learned to live in a community, and developed the art of negotiating with other household members.

For my parents, settling in a home with their parents had favourable and less favourable aspects. The favourable side was that they had childcare at home while they were at work. The less favourable side was the lack of privacy and freedom to have their own nuclear family living.

My grandparents had the advantage of active community living with their adult children and grandchildren. It was an environment where they wouldn't feel lonely. They also had a meaningful life as they took part and contributed to the household's daily activities. Everyone had their roles and contributions in our mini-community.

Each family has its own needs and relationship dynamics. A multigenerational home embodies community living. We can design the home to work for each family's needs, even with challenges such as a lack of privacy and too much noise. We can address the spatial architectural challenges and resolve them easily when we plan for them early.

The other side of the coin is the dynamics of community living that require more care, patience, and conscious effort from each member of the household—dynamics such as relationship building and respecting each other's needs and personal boundaries.

In my observation and experience, it takes commitment and unconditional love to stay together in multigenerational living. If families can work through the relational side, this way of living has excellent potential as a solution to housing affordability, because it enables multiple generations from one family to share their resources.

An ancient multigenerational home

I travelled to southern China many years ago and visited an area well known for its ancient multigenerational houses. One of the ethnic groups, the Hakka people, has an ancient tradition and method of building a rammed earth, multigenerational house called the Tulou.[13] One of those houses has survived a few hundred years and become part of the UNESCO World Heritage Sites.

The Hakka people built these houses among the mountainous terrain of the Fujian province, between Yongding and Nanjing counties in southern China. The house floor plan can be round or square, with an open courtyard in the middle.

From a bird's-eye view, the round-shaped house is like a doughnut. It is three or four storeys high, with very few windows on the second storey and above. From the outside, these houses look more like forts built among the mountains. The closest thing to it in our modern building would be a round three- or four-storey walk-up apartment building, but the shape also reminded me of the Colosseum in Rome.

The internal structure of the Tulou is of timber construction with rammed earth on the external walls, much like Australian brick veneer construction (a two-layer construction method of brickwork on the external wall and timber structure on the internal). All the Tulou's rooms face the open-air central courtyard for views and ventilation. The courtyard also contains a well, offering fresh water for the community in this enormous house. It is a self-sufficient community amid the harsh environment.

The concept and purpose of the ancient Tulou is to enable extended families to live in one compound—community living, where they share resources and support one another. It is a fascinating ancient architectural heritage of multigenerational, multi-household community living and something that seems to be returning in our modern adoption of multigenerational homes.

Community living has taken a back seat in our modern world. However, as many of us experienced in the COVID-19 pandemic, technology alone can't replace human interactions. As society experiences changes—with smaller family units, ageing populations, family breakdowns, and lack of housing affordability—the multigenerational home is a concept worth considering for some families.

Multigenerational living fosters strong family bonds, facilitates caring for the old and young, and encourages community living. It also closes the generation gap and reduces the sense of isolation prevailing in many families in our modern society.

How does a multigenerational home suit your family's lifestyle? It is a question that only you can assess.

Multigenerational homes as legacy homes

If you remember the story of James and Anna from Chapter One, they are homeowners looking to leave their home as a gift for their children.

In our current housing market, the millennial generation have less opportunity to be homeowners than their parents' generation. A multigenerational home can be a great way to create a legacy home for families who believe in passing on their home to the next generations.

A multigenerational home can be a magnificent gift to subsequent generations. It is a gift that will last a long time and will leave a legacy of memories and stories of this place that will stay in the family for many generations to come. Even if the building doesn't last in its current form, the land will last beyond one generation.

CHAPTER 7

L IS FOR LIVABLE

We have now discussed three of the Future Home's SMALL features: Smart for technology, Millennial for future living, and Adaptable for the home's ability to adapt to a homeowner's changing needs.

The fourth SMALL feature of Future Home is L for Livable

1. S<small>MART</small>
2. M<small>ILLENNIAL</small>
3. A<small>DAPTABLE</small>
4. **L<small>IVABLE</small>**
5. L<small>OW ENERGY CONSUMPTION</small>

Livable represents a home that is safe, comfortable, and easily accessible to homeowners going through different phases of their lives.

The story of Nigel and Doreen from Chapter One provides an example of some homeowners who would benefit from the Livable feature. They are an elderly couple in their 70s, looking to downsize. Nigel and Doreen's situation represents a growing theme of stories I hear from homeowners who want to downsize but find it hard to find the right home in which to grow old.

Many of our elders prefer to grow old in their homes. It is a more comfortable arrangement with less financial burden for themselves, the family, and the taxpayers. However, we have not designed most of the houses in the market to provide Livable accommodation.

Livable is a Future Home feature that benefits many homeowners, not just downsizers. Other homeowners who would benefit from this feature are:

- Families with young children where mothers need to manoeuvre prams in and out of the home
- People with temporary injuries
- People with disabilities.

Building your Future Home doesn't have to be an expensive exercise. Early planning with foresight will save homeowners tens of thousands of dollars on a major renovation or the cost of moving from home to home in the course of their lifetime.

Families experience constant change in their lives. Some changes, like raising children and growing old, are a natural part of life. Others are the result of unexpected events that we need to adapt to, such as temporary injuries or disabilities because of illness or accidents.

We live in an ageing society where people live longer because of improved quality of life and advancements in science, nutrition, and medicine. Retirement age is getting older because people can live longer and enjoy a better quality of life. Many elders can still contribute to society way after their official retirement age.

According to the Australian Bureau of Statistics, in 2017–9 the average life expectancy at birth for Australian males is 80.9 years, and for females 85 years.[14] And for Australians who make it to their retirement age of 65 years, males can expect to live until 84.9 years and females till 87.6 years.

This ever-increasing lifespan comes with a need for support and care for our elderly. Currently, the elderly can receive support and care through the aged care sector, their family members, or community-based service providers.

> **Livable represents a home that is safe, comfortable, and easily accessible to homeowners going through different phases of their lives.**

Many elders prefer to receive support from family members or community providers by remaining in their homes for as long as possible. Research shows that the elderly have a better quality of life by ageing in the comfort of their home than at the aged care facilities. It often causes emotional strain and anxiety for elderly people to move from their familiar home environment to an unfamiliar setting.

BENEFITS OF AGEING IN PLACE FOR THE ELDERLY

There are many benefits to ageing in your family home.

Healthier environment

Living in your own home is a healthier choice than living in close quarters with other elders in an aged care home. It reduces the risk of exposure to sicknesses and diseases.

Independent quality of life

Keeping your independence in your own home gives you that sense of freedom, self-sufficiency, and quality of life. You have the freedom to manage your own time to pursue your recreational activities and interact with the outside world.

Healthy, active day-to-day lifestyle

Staying in your own home supports you in your daily routine and lifestyle. An active lifestyle gives your life meaning and satisfaction.

Emotional and mental health

Staying in your own home allows you to remain connected to other people in your neighbourhood, which gives you better emotional and mental well-being.

Familiar environment

Most people feel safer and more comfortable in a familiar environment they have been in for many years. When elderly people move from their familiar environment to an unfamiliar environment or community, it often causes them emotional strain and anxiety.

Family and friends within reach

You are within closer contact and reach to your family and friends in your own home. You won't feel displaced or lonely, because the people you care about are still around you. Aged care facilities often have specific visitation times, which restrict others from visiting outside those times.

Cost-effective solution

Aged care facilities require a sizeable sum of upfront cost plus higher monthly care expenses. Staying in your home is more cost-effective, especially if you have planned your home well to include Livable features to assist ageing in your home with comfort.

> **Early planning with foresight will save homeowners tens of thousands of dollars on a major renovation or the cost of moving from home to home in the course of their lifetime.**

HOW CAN YOU PLAN TO GROW OLD IN YOUR HOME?

Homeowners planning to age in their own homes can incorporate Livable facilities and features at the start of their home building project. This avoids major renovations or the need to move to another suitable home as the need arises. It also saves on costs when you include the structural features early, rather than later when you need them.

Livable features help you move around safely in your home as you age gracefully, and they help prevent accidents and falls; as they say, prevention is better than cure. But they're not only for the elderly—Livable home features also provide a safe environment for families with young children, disabled family members, or household members with temporary injuries.

Based on Livable Housing design guidelines, there are three levels of performance and rating for livable design: silver, gold, and platinum.[15]

Silver represents entry-level performance and has seven basic core design features:

1. Safe continuous level pathway in and out of your home to the street entrance or parking area
2. At least one level (step-free) entrance into your home
3. Internal doors and corridors that provide comfortable and unrestricted movement, with a minimum clearance width of 1000 mm
4. Stepless shower recess
5. Ground-floor bathroom and toilet facilities
6. Reinforced walls around toilet and shower recesses to support the installation of grab rails when it is time to install them
7. Stairways that are safe and enable future modification.

Depending on the level of performance or rating homeowners desire to achieve—silver, gold, or platinum—they can choose from the guidelines' features to achieve that performance level.

Homeowners preparing to build their growing-old home would benefit from a single-storey instead of a two-storey home. The advantage of a single-storey home for the elderly is the easy maintenance and movement around the home. Ease of movement helps prevent falls, which can be fatal for the elderly.

If you plan to build a two-storey home, plan for all the living areas and facilities to be on the ground floor. It is also advisable to have an en suite master bedroom on the ground floor. Some homeowners will invest in a home lift, if budget permits, to provide greater comfort and ease of movement between different levels.

Other design considerations that homeowners should adopt are non-slip floors, open living spaces or visually connected spaces, and fewer sharp-corner circulation paths between spaces.

It is important to plan for and include the structural features early into the home design, including corridor width, non-slip flooring, step-free entrances, and reinforced shower walls. Homeowners can add minor changes like grab rails closer to the time when they need them.

Planning to build Future Home to grow old in is a better option than moving to an institutional care facility or finding another suitable home at a later stage. Moving is a stressful endeavour for most people, especially the elderly. It is also challenging to find a home in the market that has Livable design features.

The government increasingly encourages older Australians to grow old at home in the community rather than staying at aged care facilities. Elders living in institutions increase the national burden, whereas those living in community with their families reduce public costs.

Homeowners planning to build Future Home are investing in a future lifestyle. The longer they extend the use of their home, the more beneficial and cost-efficient it is for them and their family.

This is where Future Home features such as Smart, Millennial, Adaptable, and Livable make a big difference. A home that's adaptable as your life changes increases cost savings and return in the long run. You will see a return on your investment in your finances, comfort, wellness, and peace of mind.

In the next chapter, we will discuss the last feature of Future Home: Low energy consumption. This is a feature that has received a lot more attention in recent years. A home that has low energy consumption reduces utility costs and helps the planet.

As we reveal one feature after another, we give you a peek into future living. I trust that as we build this foundation of truth and knowledge, one block at a time, you will gain clarity in the value of building Future Home for you and your family.

CHAPTER

L IS FOR LOW ENERGY CONSUMPTION

We have finally arrived at the last SMALL feature of Future Home. And trust me—I kept the best till last!

The fifth SMALL feature of Future Home is L for Low energy consumption

1. SMART
2. MILLENNIAL
3. ADAPTABLE
4. LIVABLE
5. **LOW ENERGY CONSUMPTION**

Low energy consumption represents a home that is energy efficient and less expensive to run.

How do you keep your home warm in winter without increasing the energy bill? Is your home warm and comfortable when the outdoor temperature drops? Or do you always feel the draughty air blowing through the rooms during those cold and windy winter months?

Do you struggle to turn on the heater in winter for fear of the skyrocketing heating bill? Do you just put up with the cold by wearing layers of clothes, woollies, socks, beanies, and a shawl to keep you warm, even inside your home?

What about during the hot summer months—those days when it gets to the high 30s, even 40s Celsius? Does your home provide thermal comfort during such extreme weather? Or does the indoors have a similar temperature to the outside air, with only a couple of degrees' difference?

Low energy consumption represents a home that is energy efficient and less expensive to run.

Maybe it's not a dilemma or choice any more for you. Perhaps you have babies, toddlers, or elderly people in your home, and you need to maintain comfortable temperatures; you need to keep them warm and comfortable, or they'll fall sick. It can be a potential health hazard for the elderly and very young to stay in a cold house where the indoor temperature is below the recommended safety level. The World Health Organization recommends a minimum of 18°C for indoor room temperature.[16] The general recommended room temperature for older people and younger children is 20–21°C.

Ian and Christina's story in Chapter One represents most Australian homeowners staying in old suburban homes in Australia's southeast, where the climate is colder and harsher than in the other parts of the continent.

Ian and Christina live in a house built in the 1970s. It gets too cold in winter and too hot in summer. They have to turn on the heater all the time during winter to stay warm. A similar thing happens in summer, where they have to rely on the air conditioner in the hottest months. Their energy bill is always very high during those extreme weather months.

If Ian and Christina's story resonates with you, then you're reading the most relevant section of this book. I trust this chapter will enlighten you and empower you to take the right action moving forward.

We've all heard about energy star ratings for our household electrical appliances—the fridge, freezer, dishwasher, washing machine, air conditioner, and portable heater. The more stars the appliance has in its rating, the more energy efficient it is.

It's the same with homes in Australia: we rate them with an energy star rating. In 2003 we incorporated the minimum standard for energy efficiency into the Building Codes of Australia for residential buildings. This is good news for homeowners, as it's now compulsory for all newly built residential buildings to comply with this requirement.

From 2010 until now, all newly built homes need to meet a minimum 6-star rating (out of 10 stars) for their energy efficiency performance. The higher the star rating of your home, the more energy efficient your home is supposed to be.

A home that is energy efficient uses less energy; it is a low energy consumption home. For simplicity, we will use the terms low energy consumption home and energy-efficient home interchangeably.

Homeowners who understand the value of a highly energy-efficient home will invest in features to achieve a higher energy rating than the current regulatory requirement of 6 stars.

Some energy-efficient features are high-performance insulation (on the walls, floors, and roofs), solar panels, rainwater tanks, and double- or triple-glazed windows. These features, if installed properly, will increase the energy rating of your home. An energy consultant will work with your architect to design a home that will achieve the star rating as per the regulatory requirement—or go beyond it, if that is where you would like to invest.

However, sometimes these energy-efficient features—insulation and double-or triple-glazed windows—do not perform as they should, and they don't increase the energy rating as they should. Why is that? Most likely, they're not properly installed, and their performance wasn't checked after installation.

Sadly, this is the current situation in the Australian construction industry. To eliminate this problem of non-performing 'energy-efficient' features, homeowners, architects, and builders need to work together. Before signing the building contract, homeowners should ensure an agreement is in place to measure energy efficiency performance after construction is complete. We will reveal more of this aspect in Section Two: Industry Secrets.

WHAT ARE THE BENEFITS OF LOW ENERGY CONSUMPTION HOMES FOR HOMEOWNERS?

An energy-efficient home brings multiple benefits for you, your family, and the planet:

- Using less energy means reduced running costs for your home and savings on your energy bill.
- Thermal comfort inside your home throughout the year means lower bills and better health for the family since they are less exposed to the effects of a cold house.
- Better air quality and a healthier environment inside your home, with less dependence on mechanical heating and cooling all year round, also contribute to better health; poor indoor air quality contributes to respiratory problems, dry skin, and allergies.
- Producing fewer greenhouse emissions means you are creating a better environment for the planet, your family, and your future generations. If we look after the environment, the environment will look after us. We are part of a big ecosystem that is mutually dependent.

- It is a good financial investment. Energy bills increase every year; it is a smart investment for homeowners to prepare their home to be energy efficient and even move towards energy self-sufficiency.
- Future-proofing your home increases its resale value. Homeowners are more willing to invest in an energy-efficient home, and the demand for such homes will soon exceed the supply. As a Future Home owner, you will benefit from this trend.

There are four key components that reduce energy consumption:

1. **PASSIVE DESIGN PRINCIPLE**
2. **PASSIVE HOUSE (PASSIVHAUS) STANDARD**
3. **HIGH ENERGY RATING**
4. **AIRTIGHTNESS.**

Let's break down these key components to gain a better understanding of their benefits.

PASSIVE DESIGN PRINCIPLE

Passive design is a design principle that considers a building's orientation, taking full advantage of the sun's movement and the natural breeze to heat and cool the house. A house with passive design consideration is more comfortable to live in. It is less reliant on mechanical heating and cooling. According to the publication *Your Home, Australia Guides to Environmentally Sustainable Homes*, heating and cooling accounts for about 40% of the energy used in the average Australian home.[17] Imagine the savings you can achieve if you can leverage passive design principles to reduce your home's energy consumption.

Basic principles of passive design

- Allow the warm winter sun to come into the house.
- Keep away the scorching summer sun.

- Allow the cool breeze on summer days to flush out the hot air from the house.

Components that contribute to passive design

Orientation

Passive design considers the house's location on the land to take advantage of the sun's path and any breeze. It allows the sun to warm the house naturally in winter, while the breeze flushes hot air from the house on hot summer nights. Using these natural elements, we create a comfortable temperature in the home. This helps homeowners to be less dependent on mechanical heating and cooling and saves on their energy bills.

Shading

Passive design considers sun shading or planting to shade the house from unwanted sun in summer. Some examples of fixed shading are house eaves, shutters, and pergolas.

Thermal mass

Passive design allows high-density materials like concrete, brick, and tiles to act as thermal mass. These materials, placed in the location that catches the most sun during the day, will store the heat and slowly release it at night when it's needed.

Natural light

Passive design maximises the natural light coming into the house's different rooms and creates a healthy home, increased comfort, and a better mood for the home's occupants. It also reduces the need to use artificial lighting during the day, saving on energy consumption.

Solar panels

We are fortunate in Australia to have plenty of sunlight as clean and free energy. According to the Australian Department of Industry, Science, Energy, and Resources, as of 31 October 2020 we have installed over 2.59 million rooftop solar panels across Australia.[18] Globally, we are the highest user, with over 21% of homes having rooftop solar panels. That is good news! As the demand goes up, the price is going down. The product's technology will also get better as suppliers spend more on research and development.

Homeowners who desire to be self-sufficient in their energy supply, or are transitioning to off-grid power, might consider storing the converted solar energy in a rechargeable solar battery. Keeping the excess electricity in your own battery storage allows you to use that electricity as a backup at night or on cloudy days. It is also more profitable for homeowners to store their excess electricity than feeding it back to the main grid, as suppliers do not give a good return rate. You might, however, like to do a calculation on your usage versus the cost of the battery and the payback time. With more demand for and interest in solar batteries, the cost is becoming more affordable than when they were first launched.

Rainwater tank

Rainwater is another natural resource we can harvest to use for household utilities. In areas and months where rain is scarce, harvesting the rainwater produces an additional saving to your water bill.

We harvest rainwater from the roof runoff, connected to the water tank storage. We can use this harvested rainwater for toilet flushing and watering the garden. Depending on how well they maintain the rainwater tank, some homeowners are also comfortable using their harvested rainwater for washing clothes.

Self-sufficient rural homes in Australia depend on rainwater harvesting for their water supply, including drinking water. The benefit for these rural homes is that their rainwater is of better quality than that from the urban areas because there are fewer pollutants and chemical contamination in their surroundings.

Benefits of passive design

- Reduces reliance on mechanical heating and cooling throughout the year
- Increases natural light, which affects human mood and health
- Reduces heating and cooling bills and is cost-effective to run
- Is better for the environment and reduces the greenhouse effect
- Provides increased thermal comfort inside the home
- Makes the home healthier to live in.

Passive design considerations for different rooms

We place the sleeping zone on the cooler side of the house—which is the south-facing side for those living in the southern hemisphere.

We place the living, kitchen, and family rooms in the area of the house that receives sun throughout the day or in the morning—the north- and east-facing sides for Australia.

We place the utility zone (bathroom, toilet, laundry, garage) in the less desirable part of the house that has less sun or too much sun—the west- or south-facing sides in Australia.

Let's look at the second component that makes your home consume less energy.

PASSIVE HOUSE (PASSIVHAUS) STANDARD

We shouldn't confuse the passive design principle we just discussed with the Passive House (Passivhaus) standard. Passivhaus is a high-performance, airtight building standard originating in Germany.

The Passivhaus standard includes a rigorous building method and internationally recognised certification process. We can apply the Passivhaus standard to houses and other building types, including commercial, institutional, and educational settings.

The Passivhaus standard uses 90% less heating and cooling energy than most conventional building methods.[19] Building to Passivhaus standard certification means meeting certain criteria, methods of construction, and tests done during the construction stage.

The air coming in and out of the house is fully controlled and accounted for. There is minimal air leakage: 0.6 air changes per hour at 50 Pascals pressure (this is referred to as the ACH50 number). The lower the air change rate value, the tighter the home, and the more energy efficient it is.

A report published by the Commonwealth Scientific and Industrial Research Organisation in 2015 tested the airtightness of 125 homes around Australia and found that the average ACH50 value was 15.4.[20] So compared with the Passivhaus standard ACH50 of 0.6, Australian homes are 25 times leakier than the Passivhaus standard! These houses are mainly new houses under three years old and presumably have a 6-star energy rating. We can see from this report that a 6-star energy rating alone is no guarantee that your home is well sealed or that your energy bill will be low.

Several houses in the study—the poorly sealed houses, common among the draughty older houses—recorded air change rates above 30 ACH50. No wonder most of us have to turn on the heater all the time to keep us warm in winter, like Ian and Christina.

Passivhaus standard homes require special mechanical ventilation. The main ventilation system for the entire house uses energy recovery ventilation (ERV) or heat recovery ventilation (HRV). These recovery systems deliver fresh filtered air into the building without the draughtiness that is often an issue in older homes.

The ERV or HRV system also heats or cools the outside fresh air to a comfortable room temperature before it enters the home, creating a comfortable room temperature throughout. It also benefits household members who have respiratory problems like asthma or allergies to pollen and dust. Nevertheless, opening the windows a few times a day for a complete air exchange throughout the home is always a good practice, as in any other home.

Homeowners who build Passivhaus homes will work with a consultant who is a certified Passivhaus designer. Such a designer will advise on the Passivhaus building method to achieve the required standard for the certification process. Alternatively, homeowners can work with architects who are also certified Passivhaus designers.

The builder and tradesperson involved in the construction also need to be certified Passivhaus tradespeople, trained to build according to the Passivhaus building method, in order for the house to qualify for certification.

Passivhaus is still a very niche market among homeowners and industry professionals in Australia. The cost of building a Passivhaus home is slightly higher than that of a conventional or high-performance home. However, Passivhaus is gaining more traction and exposure in recent years as homeowners are more aware of the choices available when building high-performance homes.

In parallel to the Passivhaus standard, high-performance homes that are airtight and energy efficient are achievable. We can achieve them without the specialised team needed to build to Passivhaus standards. By understanding the different options available, homeowners can decide which features they would like to adopt and invest in.

The next component we will discuss is energy rating. How does your home's energy rating affect your energy consumption?

HIGH ENERGY RATING

The energy rating is a measurement of the house's thermal performance—the amount of heating and cooling that will be required to keep the house comfortable all year round.

Since 2011, all newly built or renovated houses in Australia have to meet the minimum energy rating of 6 stars (out of a possible 10) or its equivalent depending on the state and territory. The higher the star rating, the more thermally comfortable the home is, and the more cost-efficient it is to run.

The minimum energy-efficient rating is mandated in the National Construction Code (NCC), which is the national standard for building construction throughout Australia. During the design of your home, your architect will work with an energy assessor, a specialist consultant, to achieve the minimum 6-star rating according to the NCC requirement.

You can, of course, build your home to a higher rating than the minimum 6-star rating to achieve more energy efficiency.

How do we measure energy rating?

Software called NatHERS calculates and measures energy ratings. The software calculates the house's design intent based on the materials and construction method of the building's envelope—the roof, walls, windows, and floors. It also considers the orientation of the house, the sun shading, and the insulation used.

The energy assessor consultant determines the energy rating of your home based on the design and drawings of your architect. Your home needs to achieve the minimum energy rating of 6 stars by law in Australia as of now. If you want to achieve a higher rating than the minimum requirement, you need to inform your architect early in your project in order for them to incorporate your request in the design.

Does a high energy rating increase your home's value?

The real estate industry in Australia has not emphasised the value of high-energy-rated homes, except in the Australian Capital Territory (ACT). Since 1999, ACT is the only state in Australia where homeowners selling their homes have to provide mandatory disclosure of their home's energy efficiency rating (EER) to buyers as part of the sales transaction. The EER disclosure creates a transparent market in which everyone involved in the buying and selling of the home has information on the energy efficiency of the home. This information is used to determine the added value of the home.

In a recent study by the University of Melbourne, property lecturer Dr. Georgia Warren-Myers and University of Cambridge visiting fellow Dr. Franz Fuerst analysed tens of thousands of property transactions from 2011 to 2016 in ACT.[21] The study found that the higher the rating, the higher the selling price of the house. A 5-star-rated house will attract a 2% increase in sales price compared with a 3-star-rated house. A 6-star-rated house will increase by 2.4%, while a 7-star rating will increase the sales price by up to 9.4%.

Many real estate agents in other states in Australia are not yet fully on board with promoting energy-efficient features to homeowners. They bombard homeowners with information and education on other features with 'high selling values' and 'what buyers want'—features such as the number of bedrooms and bathrooms and other cosmetic improvements, which look impressive on the outside but may not represent a reduction in the cost of running the home.

I've heard this kind of thing often from homeowners who bought a newly renovated home: 'It's been renovated poorly with many shortcuts. We need to fix a few faulty items that were hidden and covered up at the point of sale.'

Sadly, this is a common practice in the housing industry—it's a trick of the trade that homeowners learn from the industry when it's time to sell their own houses. But this mindset breeds poor practice in the industry. As sellers, homeowners entice buyers with superficial features. However, as buyers, they will also be at the receiving end of the same poor practice conducted by their fellow homeowners who are selling.

How ironic is that? Everyone just passes on the buck to someone else. Unfortunately, what goes around comes around. Everyone ends up with the same problems and inferior products they started with.

CHAPTER EIGHT: L IS FOR LOW ENERGY CONSUMPTION

How do we break this cycle of creating homes that are not beneficial to homeowners in the long run?

I believe it is important that homeowners have a closer look at the information and advice they receive. When I ask people if they would like to live in a thermally comfortable home with a lower energy bill, nobody says no!

Given a choice, homeowners want features that benefit them as they live in their homes—features that last, not the cosmetic features that shine at the point of sale but fall apart soon afterwards.

As a seller, if you put yourselves in the shoes of the buyer, you'll want the same thing they want. Understanding the buyer's needs will position you better to highlight and sell your home. You know what benefited you, and the buyer will benefit from the same features. Your home will have a better chance of selling at a higher price too.

The house agent might not know the special features of your home that benefit you. Which part of your home gives you joy? What is the feature that has saved you most in the running cost of your home? The real estate agents need your input in selling the features that will benefit other homeowners. As a homeowner, you're in a better position to know what the market wants because you have the same mind as the buyer—your fellow homeowner.

Future Home should be a homeowners' market: by homeowners, for homeowners. Homeowners, not the real estate agents or investment gurus, create the demand and the trend. Have your say and make your voice heard. What kind of home do you want to build? What kind of home do you want to live in?

If every homeowner is onboard in cultivating this mindset and practice, I believe we will see better-quality homes for everyone to enjoy. The market is changing as homeowners realise the benefit of energy-efficient homes. The demand for this feature will also increase as a result.

What elements contribute to an energy-efficient home?

Weather sealing of the building envelope and insulation are important ways to achieve a high-energy-rating home. The building envelope is the external skin of your house—the walls, roofs, windows, floors and foundation. These are elements that protect us from the weather.

Quality materials and proper installation of the building envelope elements are equally important. Often, we hear about the use of double glazing to improve the energy rating of a home. There is some value in that; however, we can't achieve a high-energy-rated home without adequate insulation or proper sealing of the air leakage.

Insulation—a hidden element of the energy-efficient home

Homeowners who understand the benefits of a high-energy-rated home will invest to exceed the mandatory 6-star rating. Some elements that homeowners put in their homes include high R-value insulation and double- or triple-glazed windows.

Most of the information from property investors does not mention energy rating as one key to increase your house value. But as we have seen from the research done in ACT, a higher energy rating means your home will sell for a higher price.[21]

I see a conflict of interest when investors educate homeowners to build their homes as investment properties by evaluating the resale value. This plan sounds excellent at the surface level—until we look at it more closely. Consider this: investors don't live in the homes they build, nor do they pay for the utility bill. Is there any wonder they don't consider energy efficiency features?

However, as a homeowner, you live in the home you build, and you pay for the energy bill throughout the life cycle of your home. What would your consideration be? To build a home that you're comfortable living in and which has low running costs? Or to build a home with high running costs that will suit a potential buyer, if you sell your home, in maybe 10–15 years?

This information creates confusion for homeowners who are planning to build or renovate their homes. Short-term investors and real estate agents will advise homeowners to add value to things that buyers can see, like a luxurious-looking kitchen, an updated bathroom, or other shiny objects.

Have you heard advice that sounds like this: 'Don't spend on things buyers can't see' or 'Don't spend on things buyers will not pay for'?

Energy rating elements like the insulation inside your home's walls, floors, and roof space are unseen. However, their existence or non-existence affects your home. They make a difference in your thermal comfort and the cost of running your home.

Do you live in a home where you feel the heat disappear as soon as you turn off the heater—that is, your home doesn't stay warm without the heater continuously pumping? That is one symptom of a home that doesn't have enough insulation. It's like wearing thin summer clothes on a cold winter day.

Insulation is needed to achieve a high-energy-rated home that will give you a consistently comfortable temperature inside your home. You can turn on the heater to reach a certain temperature, and then the insulation will keep the heat inside the home at that same temperature for an extended period.

The value of double-glazed windows

A double-glazed window—two pieces of glass with an air gap in between—placed at the right orientation can help your home to achieve a

> **Energy rating elements like the insulation inside your home's walls, floors, and roof space are unseen. However, their existence or non-existence affects your home.**

high energy rating. The air gap between the sheets of glass acts as a thermal barrier to stop the warm air inside the house from escaping and the cold air outside from coming in.

In Section Two, we'll explore further some of the myths, truths, and secrets surrounding the method of measuring energy rating. Having the right knowledge and proper planning for building your Future Home gives you a return on your investment that is measurable and quantifiable.

This knowledge also empowers you to speak to your architect, builder and building team on achieving a higher energy rating than the minimum 6-star rating. In 2022, there is a plan for the NCC to increase the minimum energy rating to 7 stars, so Future Home owners might like to consider moving past the minimum 6-star rating to prepare for future NCC compliance.

As a nation, we are continually improving our homes' energy efficiency to reduce carbon emissions and help homeowners save on their energy bills. What is your priority? What kind of home would you like to build and live in?

AIRTIGHTNESS

Let's start with a definition. *Airtightness*, as it relates to buildings, is the resistance to inward or outward air leakage through unintentional leakage points or areas in the building envelope.[22]

The key phrase in the definition above is 'air leakage through unintentional leakage points or areas in the building envelope'. In this section, we'll look at real-life examples of airtightness in a home.

What is a leaky-air home?

Most old houses in Australia are draughty and leaky.

Remember the story of Ian and Christina in Chapter One? Their 1970s home is cold in winter and hot in summer. They can't keep it at a comfortable temperature without constantly turning on the heating or cooling, depending on the season. That's the symptom of a leaky-air home—a home built without airtightness in mind.

We looked at the Passivhaus standards earlier in this chapter. Passivhaus is a high-performance, airtight building standard. The air going in and out of the house is fully controlled or accounted for; there should be no air leaks from any gaps or holes around the building envelope, the floors, the walls, or the roof. This way, the house can perform to its optimal capacity to heat and cool the interior using very little energy.

As with the Passivhaus standard, an airtight home will stay warm in winter from the body heat and activities inside the house, with additional mechanical heating if needed, while the cold air outside will stay outside. In summer, the house will stay cool without the hot air from outside going inside or the cool air from inside escaping to the outside.

A leaky and draughty house is not comfortable to live in and is expensive to run because of the energy wasted through the unintentional leaks in the building envelope. Airtightness is important for all homes—not just for Passivhaus homes—because it affects the home's energy efficiency.

Imagine how much energy is lost when your home has holes around the windows and doors, the junctions of walls and floors, behind the joinery in your kitchen, not to mention all the exhaust fans, fireplace chimneys, ventilation outlets, and penetrations of services and pipes. That could amount to an extensive area of your home being exposed to the outside air. Having this many air holes is like leaving open a few of your home's windows or doors constantly throughout the seasons.

What are the benefits of airtight homes?

- **THERMAL COMFORT ALL YEAR ROUND**—Airtight homes stay warm in winter and cool in summer.

- **LOWER ENERGY BILL**—An airtight home prevents unintentional air leaks and energy leaks, lowering your energy bill.
- **HEALTHY HOME AND BETTER AIR QUALITY**—An airtight home prevents dust, bugs, pests, and pollen from entering through those unsealed cracks and holes. Depending on how tightly sealed your home is, however, you may need to install mechanical ventilation to prevent condensation and provide fresh air into the home.
- **BETTER FOR THE ENVIRONMENT**—Airtight homes use less energy, thus reducing greenhouse gas emissions, which helps the environment.

How can we make our home airtight?

Airtightness has been missing in most Australian houses.

The measurement of airtightness using blower door tests has not been part of the construction process except for Passivhaus-certified homes.

John and Fay's story

John and Fay live in a 1980s suburban home in Australia. Like Ian and Christina, their home feels draughty in winter, and they have to turn the heater on to keep the house warm. John and Fay were looking to upgrade their home's windows to solve this problem. They did some research, and the window suppliers advised them to replace a few windows in their home with double glazing as the solution.

It sounded like a reasonable solution, except for one thing. The window suppliers hadn't done a complete assessment for leaky home symptoms. How would they know if the windows were the only area of air leakage?

What John and Fay needed was a blower door test before going ahead with the window replacement. This test is like getting a doctor's diagnosis for leaky home symptoms. Getting the right diagnosis is an important step before prescribing the correct treatment; without an accurate diagnosis, we get the wrong medication, and that could be fatal or a waste of our time and money.

Unfortunately, following the window suppliers' advice, John and Fay skipped the diagnosis and went directly to the prescribed treatments. They falsely assumed that the windows were the only problem area in their home. They thought the airtightness test would be an unnecessary expense on top of the double-glazed windows.

At the end of the upgrade exercise, thousands of dollars later, one room still felt draughty and cold as soon as the heater was off. John and Fay are considering installing floor insulation as the next remedy.

What happens if, after the floor insulation upgrade, they still can't achieve a satisfactory result? What happens if, besides poor flooring insulation, a big hole behind the cabinet leaks air? It sounds like a cat chasing after its own tail, doesn't it?

We can't get to the bottom of the issue without a proper diagnosis. Without the proper test, you'll spend more money than you need on trial-and-error remedies that might not even fix the problem. Is it worth your money and time to take that kind of risk?

If your home is the biggest investment in your life, I recommend calculating the cost of the blower door test in relation to the current market value of your home. A blower door test will cost a few hundred dollars, depending on the size of your home. What is your home's market value—a few hundred thousand? Is it worth paying less than 1% of your home's value to get the right diagnosis to achieve the correct remedies?

The right diagnosis and remedies offer thermal comfort and cost savings throughout the life of your home. With those savings every year, how long before you can recoup the few hundred dollars it cost for the test? Isn't that worth your investment?

You will also benefit from thermal comfort if you get an accurate diagnosis of the problem. Thermal comfort means less reliance on mechanical heating and cooling. Does that add value to your health and well-being? Does it give you a saving on your heating and cooling bill?

I trust that, as a well-informed homeowner, you will assess and make decisions that benefit you and your family as the primary beneficiaries of your home. Many homeowners have adopted the mindset of short-term investors through the influence of the real estate industry's advice and investment gurus. But I know through my research that investment property and residential property are not in the same world. They exist separately.

Homeowners should not mix the two, or get confused about which hat they're wearing. Are you a homeowner or an investor? You can't wear both hats at the same time. As we have seen from the examples of energy efficiency features, there is a conflict of interest between investors' and homeowners' views. Who is paying the cost of running your home?

Homeowners who treat their home as an investment property will miss out on the long-term return on investment and the enjoyment of their home. Likewise, if you treat your investment property as your home, you will spend too much capital relative to your personal preference and emotional attachment. You won't be an effective investor.

Beware of the generic, one-size-fits-all solution. Remember John and Fay, who replaced a few of their windows with double glazing but still didn't fully achieve the improvement they paid for. They didn't get the results they were led to expect by the window suppliers.

We will explore more about energy efficiency rating and airtightness myths, truths and secrets in the next section, Industry Secrets.

That brings us to the end of the first section, and I trust you have gained some useful insights into Future Home's SMALL features. Whether you're a homeowner in Australia or another part of the world, apart from the specific regulations, I believe many design principles and industry secrets are very similar and universally applicable.

You can download the summary of SMALL in the Bonus section for a handy reference. The summary will give you a quick overview of all the features, the benefits, and how to apply them.

Section Two
INDUSTRY SECRETS

CHAPTER

ENERGY RATING

As we discussed in Chapter Eight, a high-energy-rated home means your home consumes less energy. The higher the star rating of your home, the more energy efficient it is. A high-energy-rated home benefits from year-round thermal comfort, offers cost-efficient energy bills, and is environmentally friendly.

This chapter discusses the current industry practice for measuring energy rating and how it affects homeowners.

INDUSTRY SECRET #1: The Truth About The Energy Rating Measurement In Australia

The higher the star rating, the more efficient and better performing the home is in its energy consumption.

But that's only half the truth!

The above statement is accurate only in the ideal world of perfect conditions without human errors and real-life performance measurement after we build the house.

In reality, we base the energy star rating for all the newly built homes in Australia—the current minimum 6-star rating—on the design intent but not on real-life performance.

We calculate the energy rating using the NatHERS software by inputting the data from the architectural drawings. That's right: we base the energy rating calculation on the drawings the architects specified at the design stage—the building's orientation, materials for the building, and insulation. Based on those data, the energy assessor inputs them into the NatHERS software to calculate the expected energy rating of the house.

In short, a NatHERS energy rating is as good as a promissory note. It's just a rating of how we expect the house to perform, not the actual performance of the house once it's built.

This lack of verification during and after construction causes a loophole in the execution. Improper installation of a weatherproof membrane, missing insulation or irregular insulation installation, shoddy workmanship with unsealed holes, and air leaks around the building's envelope can all affect the home's real-life performance.

These intentional or unintentional poor construction practices will jeopardise the energy rating that was so carefully planned and calculated by NatHERS at the design stage. The software calculation makes assumptions based on the perfect installation of those building elements and other human errors during construction.

These are the setbacks and loopholes in our current regulatory practice when measuring energy efficiency; homeowners do not have the guarantee and certainty that their house will perform to the rating prescribed and intended by the architect.

It was a shocking truth to me when I first realised this! Here I am, a building professional, and I didn't realise this truth and connect the dots until recently.

HOW DO WE OVERCOME THIS DISCREPANCY?

Unless we test a home's energy efficiency performance during and after construction, an energy rating conducted at the design stage might not live up to what it promises.

A 6-star rated house, according to NatHERS, might not perform as a 6-star rated home in actual life. This is especially true when the house is leaky with unsealed cracks and holes or has missing insulation.

Currently, the 2019 NCC doesn't specify a follow-up process to confirm the energy rating after construction. This creates discrepancies between the energy rating on paper versus the house's actual performance.

This lack of specified direction from the authorities and regulatory bodies like NCC creates a void, where we leave checking and validating—during and after construction—to the building practitioners, the architects, builders, tradespeople, and building surveyors/certifiers, to self-regulate. This doesn't guarantee a consistent and measurable result.

Here are my recommended steps for homeowners:

1. Include thorough inspections of the installation of building envelope elements during construction. Take the initiative by raising this issue with your architect and the rest of the building team at the start of your project. Make your team accountable to do thorough inspections during the construction and installation of the weatherproof membrane and insulation, and the sealing up of all air gaps around the building envelope.

> **Unless we test a home's energy efficiency performance during and after construction, an energy rating conducted at the design stage might not live up to what it promises.**

2. Include air leakage testing during construction. This should be done using the blower door test as a measurable and quantifiable verification process. Discuss the air infiltration rate you want to achieve with your architect and the blower door test specialist.

Like the minimum 6-star rating for energy efficiency measurement, there is a recommended air infiltration rate as well. But unlike the star rating, the higher the air infiltration rate, the worse your home's performance.

The current (2019) NCC recommends less than $10m^3/hr/m^2$ at 50Pa. Even though NCC states the recommended air infiltration rate, it is not a mandatory measurement, unlike the mandatory minimum 6-star energy rating.

As I mentioned in the previous chapter, air leakage will affect your home's energy efficiency. If you want to improve the energy performance of your home, you need to consider achieving a low air infiltration rate. We will discuss air leakage in more depth in the next chapter.

CHAPTER 10

AIR LEAKAGE

WHAT IS A LEAKY-AIR HOME?

Do you have a house that is draughty in winter? Do you have to turn on the heater all the time to keep warm? Do you have to choose between paying a high energy bill to keep yourself warm in winter or putting up with the cold? What about in summer? Does your home feel as hot as the outside air temperature on the high 30s and 40s Celsius days?

If you answered yes to any of the questions above, chances are your home is leaky or suffering from cold house syndrome. This means you have gaps and cracks around your home where air leaks from inside your home to outside and vice versa.

As we discussed in Chapter Eight, the definition of building airtightness is the resistance to inward or outward air leakage through unintentional leakage points or areas in the building envelope.[22] Those gaps around your home create unintentional leakage points. It is also difficult and expensive to heat leaky-air homes.

A leaky-air home is uncomfortable because of its temperature fluctuations. In the winter, your home can't contain the warm air; you will feel the draught of cold air as soon as you turn off the heater. In the summer, your home can't stop the hot air from seeping in. Your energy bill will skyrocket in the winter and hot summer months.

A home that is not properly airtight can be a potential health hazard for older people, babies, and the unwell. It places physiological stress on their body systems. Leaky-air homes are also likely to be damp, which encourages mould growth and causes respiratory problems.

Do you remember the story of John and Fay in Chapter Eight? They have a draughty home, and they received advice to change some of their windows to double-glazed ones. However, despite their investment, they still feel the draught when they turn off the heater.

John and Fay's home is more than likely one of those leaky-air homes commonly found in the Australian housing market, especially in houses built over 10 years ago. Their problems could also be caused by a combination of missing insulation and air leakage. We can assess both of these potential issues by conducting a blower door test for air leakage and thermal imaging for detecting missing insulation.

INDUSTRY SECRET #2

Many people think high-energy-rating homes do not have air leakage problems.

Here is the truth:

Air leakage affects energy efficiency and reduces the star rating of your home.

Without testing the air leakage of your home, even a 6-star-rated home, according to NatHERS, might not perform as a 6-star home; for example, see the report by CSIRO on their House Energy Efficiency Inspections Project.[20]

Even though we know airtightness is an important factor affecting energy efficiency, air leakage testing is not mandatory in the current National Construction Code (NCC 2019).

HOW DOES THIS TRUTH AFFECT HOMEOWNERS?

Every new home in Australia needs to achieve a 6-star energy rating as measured by the NatHERS tool. This specific measured outcome for energy rating leaves no wriggle room for variable interpretation by anyone in the building industry. It protects homeowners from receiving anything less than the code specifies. The only setback, as discussed in the previous chapter, is the absence of any post-construction performance-based testing to prove a home's rating.

Unlike the energy rating, NCC 2019 recommended air leakage testing as one way to verify the sealing of the building envelope. However, it is not the only way, and it is not a mandatory requirement under the code.

My years of experience in the industry have taught me how important it is for homeowners to be aware that any requirement that is not mandatory is less likely to be implemented.

Air leakage testing using a blower door test is not a process your building professionals' team will include or even be aware of under NCC 2019. But as an informed homeowner, you have the advantage of having this knowledge under your belt. It is up to you, the homeowner, to call for this process if your building team is not aware of this performance-based testing.

The code gives you a platform to ask for this verification process. You can refer

Without testing the air leakage of your home, even a 6-star-rated home, according to NatHERS, might not perform as a 6-star home

to NCC 2019 Volume 2, V2.6.2.3, p.70, where the recommended air change rate is below 10 m^3/hr/m^2@50Pa or equivalent to less than 10ACH@50Pa.[23]

Here is what the excerpt from NCC 2019 says:

> V2.6.2.3 Verification of building envelope sealing
>
> Compliance with P2.6.1(f) is verified when a building envelope is sealed at an air permeability of not more than 10m^3/h/m^2@50Pa reference pressure when tested in accordance with AS/NZS ISO 9972 Method 1
>
> Explanatory information
>
> The intent is that 10m^3/h/m^2@50Pa is broadly equivalent to 10 air changes per hour at 50Pa when applied to homes. It should be noted that V2.6.2.3 is only one way of achieving compliance with P2.6.1(f). Other ways of complying include the following:
>
> (a) The relevant provisions of Part 3.12.3.
>
> (b) A Performance Solution that uses one of the other NCC Assessment Methods, which verifies that compliance with P2.6.1(f) will be achieved.

WHY DO WE NEED TO KEEP OUR HOMES AIRTIGHT?

Air leakage accounts for 15–25% of winter heat loss and significant loss of coolness in hot weather, according to Your Home.[24] We can see the benefit of having an airtight home and the relation between airtightness and energy efficiency.

According to research conducted by CSIRO for 129 new homes of three to ten years old across the states in Australia, the average airtightness is 15.7 ACH@50Pa.[20] Some older houses have an air change rate of above 30 ACH@50Pa. This shows poor performance even for those newly built homes, which supposedly have a 6-star energy efficiency rating!

HOW DOES OUR CURRENT AIRTIGHTNESS MEASUREMENT COMPARE TO THE WORLD'S?

If you remember our Passivhaus standards discussion, the Passivhaus building method uses blower door tests to measure the home's air leakage. The air change rate required to achieve Passivhaus certification is 0.6ACH@50Pa—that's over 26 times more airtight than the national average of 15.7 ACH@50Pa.

You might say Passivhaus is too high a standard compared with other housing standards. How does our standard in airtightness compare to the rest of the world?

The UK, USA, and European countries use blower door tests as mandatory verification processes to measure airtightness for residential homes. The UK requirement for new residential buildings' airtightness is 10 ACH@50Pa; the standard in the USA and Canada is 3–5 ACH@50Pa; while the standards in most European countries range from 3 to 4 ACH@50Pa. Germany has two sets of prescription: 1.6 ACH@50Pa (mechanical ventilation) or 3.2 ACH@50Pa (natural ventilation).[25]

The above data illustrate that Australia's airtightness standard is behind that of most other countries. Airtightness not only affects the energy efficiency of the houses we build, but it also affects the overall quality of the houses we build.

WHAT CAN HOMEOWNERS DO TO SET THE INDUSTRY STANDARD?

A leaky home shows a poor level of workmanship and a poor skill set. Those cracks and gaps around the envelope of the houses are 'unnecessary features'. Bigger leaks can come from plumbing and electrical service penetrations in our homes. Some gaps even create holes big enough for rats, possums, and creepy crawlies to enter and infest our homes. It makes little sense for us to build such poor-quality homes in this 21st century, where technology and innovations are so advanced.

The feasibility of having an airtight home, as measured by a blower door test, shows the level of quality that the industry can and should deliver. It also places accountability on the building professionals to deliver to homeowners what they have paid for.

It doesn't cost builders or tradespeople extra to build an airtight home. Homeowners pay for insulation, thermal barrier, windows, and all the materials for the envelope or skin of their homes, and ultimately it is up to the tradespeople they employ to implement these resources effectively. The building code has taken the initial step to prescribe the minimum building standard. It is now up to homeowners, the consumers, to enforce the application.

Let the building professionals hear your voice. What type of home do you want to live in? What level of quality do you expect? What level of service, workmanship, and skill do you want the industry to provide?

As a Future Home owner, you are at the forefront in creating demands that will change the industry's culture and mindset to supply better homes for you and people like you. Future Home owners are the trendsetters for the market.

It's not up to the real estate industry or the investment property gurus to tell people what type of home they should live in or what is desirable to homeowners; the industry responds to market demand and trends. The industry professionals exist to serve homeowners. We are here to serve your needs, giving you what you pay for and what you deserve: a better-quality home for you and your family.

As I wrote in Chapter One, home is one of the basic human needs, regardless of our culture, upbringing, or country. Everyone needs a place to call home.

CHAPTER

OVERCAPITALISING

Overcapitalising is one of the main contentions and dilemmas homeowners face when they think of building or upgrading their homes.

WHAT IS OVERCAPITALISING?

According to the Merriam-Webster Dictionary, the definition of overcapitalise is 'to capitalise beyond what the business or the profit-making prospects warrant'.[26]

To relate the above definition to a home, overcapitalising means you invest more in your home than its actual market value. If you are building your home, the value of your investment is the value of the land plus the cost of building the house.

To illustrate this in a simplified example, say you purchase land that costs $300,000, and the estimated cost to build the new home is $500,000. That makes the total investment value for your new home $800,000. If the market value of a similar home in that area is $700,000, then you have overcapitalised on your home building project, *providing you are going to sell the home straight after you build it.* That's the caveat most homeowners forget—the timing of selling your home.

If you are not planning to sell your home after building, there is time for the property value to go up while you enjoy your newly built home. As a homeowner, it is not likely that you will build your home to sell straight away; if you do that, you are more of an investor or developer. As such, the overcapitalisation calculation we did earlier is not valid because it leaves out the home's value over time.

You need to consider the amount of time you plan to stay in your home and the average capital growth of similar homes in your area to determine whether you are overcapitalising. That can be a complicated calculation and analysis.

I spoke to a property expert who explained that they make assumptions on the expected value in the future based on historical data. Nobody knows the exact price you can expect to sell for in the future, not even the experts. However, if you are a homeowner practising due diligence and prudence, it's worth getting advice from an independent property expert. This way, you set your budget on a solid foundation. You won't be swayed by other people's opinions or what the naysayers say about overcapitalising or budgeting.

CHALLENGES OF OVERCAPITALISING AND BUDGETING FOR YOUR DREAM HOME

The number one question or challenge homeowners have is: 'How do I build my dream home without overcapitalising?'

The number two question is: 'How much will it cost to build my dream home?'

I hear both questions all the time!

Here are more variations of the questions around those two popular topics, which I've collected over the years:

- Is it worth building a dream home?
- Am I going to get a return on my investment?

- Isn't it more expensive to build my own home?

Those questions can hinder and discourage many people who are thinking of building their own home. It also doesn't help when homeowners hear about so many horror stories and disasters—budget overruns, runaway builders, project delays, or unfinished projects—all of which can lead to overcapitalisation.

From my observations, most of those disastrous stories come from homeowners who are building their homes as DIY or semi-DIY projects, managing the project themselves with the bare minimum of professional advice and a skeletal team of experts.

These homeowners usually fall into one of two common traps.

In the first one, they rely on their own knowledge and self-education, thinking they can save the cost of engaging a team of professionals. As a result, disasters and design mishaps happen. Some examples I've heard include a toilet space too small to fit a normal-size toilet suite or corner cabinet doors that can't open properly because the design didn't allow enough space. Or strange things like having to pass through the laundry area from a bedroom to reach the front door. Yes, those are examples of DIY renovations gone totally wrong!

It's amazing the risks some homeowners take and what they subject themselves to. Unfortunately, some of those mishaps create permanent damage. They cost more to fix than the DIY savings the homeowners believed they were making.

Imagine if you were going to sell that unit or house. How much have you devalued your house despite its great location? Your DIY mistakes will be a great bargaining point for the buyer. That is ironic and sad, isn't it?

In the second trap, homeowners put their trust in one person instead of a team of experts. This one person convinces the homeowner that they are the only expert needed to do the job.

Many times I've heard of homeowners' confusion over the role of the different professionals in the industry. Homeowners don't know who they should approach first when they want to build or renovate their home. Some say they met a project manager or a builder who offers a 'free design service'.

Homeowners often do not realise each consultant is an expert in their specific field. For example, builders receive training in building and construction. They can read construction drawings and build according to what the drawings prescribe. The drawings represent the homeowner's wishes, ideas, and aspirations, as translated by the architect.

But a builder is not trained to design like an architect. Architects put together the homeowner's needs and regulatory requirements and provide a creative and workable design solution to meet the client's aspirations and goals. Architects use the drawing as a blueprint or roadmap to communicate those ideas and design intent to the builder.

Other consultants, such as engineers, land surveyors, and energy consultants, give input in their own areas of expertise and work with architects and builders. It takes teamwork and cooperation from all parties to achieve the homeowner's goal. That is the value of homeowners having a team, not a single individual, to guide and help build their dream home into a reality.

Building a home, no matter how small or big, requires multiple experts. These experts ensure your dream will not turn into a nightmare. Don't let your life's savings or investment in a significant asset go to waste. I'm heartbroken when I hear this has happened.

As professionals, we know what it takes to get the job done. We know the high risks it entails. Yet those we serve do not heed our advice or trust us. And they end up in the hole, just like we knew they would. It is not something we want to celebrate or say, 'I told you so, and you didn't believe me'.

Unfortunately, that is often what we face or hear in our industry. It gives a bad rap to our profession, even though most of those incidents don't involve architects. Only a small percentage of homes in Australia are architect-designed: an estimate of 5–10%, according to an article from *The Design Files*.[27]

If you needed major surgery, you wouldn't just expect your general practitioner to perform the operation. You'd need a team of expert physicians trained on different parts of your body to do it, because each part of your body is intricately connected and affects the other parts. And it's the same when you're building a home. There are many parts to the building process, and each part is an area that someone has the knowledge and expertise to handle. The end goal is for the team to put everything together that represents the homeowner's aspirations and dreams.

THE TRUTH ABOUT OVERCAPITALISING

For years, many property investment gurus and real estate agents have bombarded homeowners with promising information, statements, and claims. They teach homeowners to be savvy investors with their own homes. These industry professionals say they have your best interests at heart. They all claim you can trust them.

I get it! I have been in this industry long enough to know its darker side. It frustrates and upsets me as much as it does you.

What I would like to do in this chapter is to present the myth, truth, and industry secrets about overcapitalising. I base this presentation on my research findings and analysis as an architect. My findings are from my years of interactions with homeowners, reading property investing materials, just like you, and speaking to people from other industry disciplines.

It is my heart's desire to present these findings so that you will have clarity on the truth of the matter. You can then arrive at your own assessment of what works for your unique situation. My goal is to empower you and entrust you with your own decisions.

I believe in tailor-made solutions because we are unique individuals. Your family, your lifestyle, and your values differ from those of other homeowners. There is no one-size-fits-all solution. Many homeowners fall into the trap of accepting a generic solution or statement, which can be just a myth. We, as humans, like to hear what we like to hear. However, truth doesn't always work that way.

I want to debunk the mystery of overcapitalising in this chapter as best I can.

Here is the myth we often hear about overcapitalising:

- Building your own home will risk overcapitalising.

As you can appreciate from our examples and discussion above, building your own home doesn't always mean you will risk overcapitalising. Planning and setting your budget helps you avoid overcapitalisation.

Here is the truth about overcapitalising:

- Homeowners can prevent overcapitalising if they manage the project with proper research, planning, and budgeting.

INDUSTRY SECRET #3

- Time is the homeowners' friend for reducing the risk of overcapitalising.

We have discussed this in the previous two chapters on energy rating and air leakage. We learned that to make your home energy efficient and airtight, you need to invest in features like insulation, double- or triple-glazed windows, and blower door tests to check the airtightness.

Those things are not what the property investors or real estate agents would advise you to invest in. They would probably say that you will overcapitalise your home if you invest in things that are 'not seen' rather than the visible things buyers will pay for. But here is the twist to that advice!

There are different reasons why homeowners want to build their own homes, and I would divide them into three categories:

1. Those who plan to build a home for the shorter term—less than seven years—and plan to sell it after that and move to another home.

2. Those who plan to build for a long-term purpose, to improve their quality of life, their family life, and even to leave a legacy for the next generation.
3. Those who plan to build a growing-old home.

If you are a homeowner who falls under the first category, building a home for short-term use, then overcapitalising should be the first and main consideration when setting your budget. You need to work closely with the property expert to determine the investment you want to put into your project. Set your budget right from the start, and stick to it when you work with your architect.

For homeowners who fall under categories two and three, though, overcapitalising might not apply because of the home's long-term purpose. The more relevant and pressing issue is your budget. How much are you planning to put into the project? Do your brief and requirements match your budget? We will discuss budget further in this chapter.

Let's consider homeowners like Mike and Heather, whose primary driver for building their home is improving their quality of life and family life. Mike and Heather have two young children, ages seven and nine, and live in an Australian suburban home. Their house was built in the 1970s and has many problems: condensation that creates damp interior walls on rainy days, a roof that leaks during heavy rain, mould in multiple rooms, and dark rooms with not enough sunlight.

> 'It has become unhealthy for us to live in this home. We don't want the children to have health issues. We want to provide them with a home that they can grow up in and enjoy. We like this area, so building our own home on the same land is a logical decision for us. It's close to the children's school, and we will enjoy the new home in the same neighbourhood that we are used to.
>
> 'It also doesn't cost us any more to build a home on our own land than if we move to another house in this area. Plus, we can't find a home that suits our needs and lifestyles in this area. We have over 10 years to enjoy this new home and see the children grow up happily, which is

worth our efforts and investment. We're investing in our family's lives and the children's future, health, and well-being.

'We put a lot of research and planning into this home-building project. We also involved the children in the project, which gets them really excited. It is a special memory that the children will have forever. The new home is something that we will enjoy as a family for many years to come.'

For Mike and Heather, building a new home is primarily about improving their family's quality of life. They never worried about overcapitalising because they set a budget for their building project and they are building the home for long-term enjoyment. They don't plan to sell it any time soon.

It is a smart decision for Heather and Mike to build in a good growth area and on their own land for a long-term purpose. Their anticipation of living in the new home for many years reduces their risk of overcapitalising. Historically, most houses in major cities increase in price over time. Understanding the area where you will build—through doing due diligence and seeking advice from property experts—will help you make an informed decision on your building project.

Time is indeed the homeowner's friend for reducing the risk of overcapitalising.

THE PREJUDICE ABOUT OVERCAPITALISING

I observe that property investors offer a lot of information, teachings, and articles on overcapitalising. Those articles lean towards viewing your home as a short-term investment rather than an owner-occupied Future Home.

This advice on overcapitalisation is not always applicable to Future Home owners. Property investors have very different mindsets and calculations over the investment they put in their building projects. Their mindset is short term and profit driven.

These are some of the questions you might like to assess. Would investors use quality materials and workmanship at the expense of maximum profit? If you are a property investor, would you live in a home built as an investment property? Would you build to the same standard and quality in a property investment home as you would in your own home?

Take the features of energy efficiency, such as insulation and airtightness. Why do you think property investors don't advise on those things? Could it be because they want to appeal to whatever catches the buyer's eye on the first inspection day? Things that buyers can see? Could it be that once they sell, they don't have to live in those homes—homes that can be draughty, thermally uncomfortable, and costly to run?

Those are questions that homeowners need to dig deeper into before taking any advice on the surface level. Do these people have the same values and needs as homeowners? Do they have other interests at stake in their advice? Is their advice impartial?

Understanding the motivation of the individuals giving the advice helps you to know who you should listen to and seek advice from. It's important to seek trusted information that empowers you to make your own assessment and decision.

RESPONSES TO THE FEAR OF OVERCAPITALISING

Overcapitalising is a term used extensively in the building industry, especially by property investors and real estate agents. They caution and warn homeowners who are planning to build or renovate their homes about it.

As we saw with Mike and Heather, overcapitalising isn't always an issue. Homeowners who plan to build for long-term purposes have as their primary goal—their WHY—enhancing their family's life and well-being. They set a comfortable project budget at the start of the build and don't worry about the resale value when and if they sell their home years later.

Misunderstanding the nuances between short-term and long-term purposes creates a fear factor in many homeowners. It grips them to the point of inaction, and keeps them frozen in their tracks.

I have met many homeowners caught in a dilemma between fulfilling their desire to build their dream home and their fear of overcapitalising. It is tragic to see many homeowners let go of their dreams, quality of life, and the opportunity to grow their asset in the long term because of this unnecessary fear.

> **It's important to seek trusted information that empowers you to make your own assessment and decision.**

From my observations over the years, homeowners will respond in two ways when they're afraid of overcapitalising.

The first response

Homeowners will delay the decision to do something with their home. They put up with the current home's condition, even if it isn't ideal. Here is how the scenario might play out in your life.

While you are delaying your decision, time passes and family life changes. Your children grow up and leave home, and you and your partner become empty nesters. The home you live in hasn't really served you well throughout your family life changes. Now you feel stuck. You have compromised all these years. What can you do now? Now, more than ever, it seems too late to do anything.

You love the area you live in, so you're reluctant to move out. Plus, as time goes by, property prices are going up everywhere, and all the places you would like to move to are more expensive than your current home. You can't afford it. Your other options aren't great, either. You don't want to trade your current home for one that is further from good infrastructure, lifestyle, and family, or for a smaller home, which is not necessarily in any better condition than where you live now.

By this time, your current home is getting older, run-down, and in need of maintenance and updating. Yet you're at the age where you don't want to go through the pressure of moving or looking for another home.

The second response

In fear of overcapitalising, some homeowners will find homes that have gone through renovation and updating. They prefer not to take the risk of building or renovating a home themselves and opt for a ready-made, done-for-you home. It is a logical solution—in a perfect world. Unfortunately, that is not how the housing market has evolved.

I spoke to a family who moved into such a home and found the renovation work was poorly done. They now have to spend more money to rectify the shoddy renovation job done by the previous owners.

Think back to our discussion on what homeowners learn from the short-term investor gurus and real estate agents: invest in cosmetic renovations to appeal to buyers' eyes. As the saying goes, cosmetic renovation is only skin-deep beauty.

What has the fear of overcapitalising done? How sad are those scenarios above?

What happens if you decide early in your life to invest in Future Home, a home that adapts to your life changes? You can stay for the long term in a home that meets your needs, and enjoy it. Whatever investment you put into the home would pay itself back. The home's value would go up because you are leveraging the increasing land value. You will also enjoy living in a home designed to meet your needs without expensive utility bills.

One thing I notice is that most homeowners don't like to move from one house to another. We are creatures of comfort. It is also not wise to keep moving home. Imagine the cost of moving homes many times in your life. It adds up: mover's cost, agent's fee, taxes, and bank fees. Try to multiply that by two for every move! Remember, once you move out of your home, you need to buy another home to live in. If you move a few times in your lifetime, how much extra cost would that be? You could put those costs to better use by investing in building one Future Home that you can live in for as long as possible.

Time is the homeowners' friend! Property values go up with time because of the land value, as we discussed in Chapter Five. While leveraging the land value increase, you enjoy your home and benefit from its use. You increase the life cycle of your home.

You benefit from living in a home that enhances your family's health and well-being, that fosters good bonding and relationships for your family life, and that provides thermal comfort where utilities are cost-efficient. You want a home you can grow old in comfortably.

Here is another scenario: as a homeowner's need to find a replacement home increases, they'll have no choice but to act. Unfortunately, with the current housing stock, they'll end up moving to a home that is not necessarily better than their previous one. The new home also needs improvement to adapt to the next phase of their life.

Where does this leave homeowners? Again, with the newly bought home, you feel stuck with this fear of overcapitalising if you want to do any home improvement work.

The old fear of overcapitalising keeps on following uninformed homeowners wherever they go. How many dreams and hopes for a better quality of life have been crushed by this fear of overcapitalising and reluctance to invest in a quality home?

Most times, homeowners don't base this fear on any logical reasoning. When I ask people whether they have done their research or financial planning on what they consider overcapitalising, most of them can't give me an answer. It is also not surprising that when I ask them what their budget is to avoid overcapitalising, they can't answer that either. The only response I receive is: 'We don't want to overcapitalise'.

PRINCIPLES TO AVOID OVERCAPITALISING

Is there a way out of the fear of overcapitalising?

Yes! I believe there is. Meeting homeowners who fear overcapitalising or are unable to set their budget has prompted me to do more research to find solutions that homeowners can adopt. I spoke to people in the property planning industry, which has helped me design a framework that I would like to share with you.

It is not a one-size-fits-all solution, but it is a framework that you can consider and apply to your unique situation. It's a starting point. And let's not forget to also follow up with tailor-made advice from the experts.

Most homeowners will do one of the following to their home: renovate and extend the existing home, build new on vacant land, or knock down and rebuild on their existing land.

For renovation and extension projects

If you plan to renovate and extend, contact a registered valuer and get valuations for your existing home and valuations for the home post-renovation based on the plans. A registered valuer or property consultant gives independent advice because they do not sell or buy properties; hence they have no conflict of interest. When you have both valuations, the before and after, you can set your budget confidently to avoid overcapitalising.

Remember to consider your time frame, too. How long do you plan to live in your newly renovated home? As we discussed earlier, property values go up over time in most major cities. If you know the data for population growth, economic growth, and the socioeconomic profile of the area, you can make an informed decision and plan your budget to avoid overcapitalising. Surrounding yourself with experts who give you the right advice is a wise move.

Independent advice is a service where the consultant receives payment for the expert research, analysis, and advice they provide. Beware of property consultants who offer 'free advice'—this often comes with strings attached. Check out whether there is a commission fee embedded in their promise of free advice and the terms and conditions of their service. If they receive commissions from a third party who sells homes to homeowners, then the purity of their advice could be tainted. You can imagine: 2–3% commission for hundreds of thousands of dollars in property sales, compared with a few hundred or thousand dollars of consultancy fee. It will detract the person's focus and allegiance!

Homeowners often have the mindset that paid professional advice is an expense they would rather avoid. Let that not be a stumbling block. Think of paid independent advice as an investment. It reduces your risk of making the wrong decision, and it is your insurance policy.

You wouldn't want to risk overcapitalising your home, which would jeopardise your hundreds of thousands of dollars' investment. You also do not want to live a 'status quo' life for 10 or 20 years in a home that doesn't serve your needs and is costly to run.

I've come across articles written by property investors who share their knowledge of costly mistakes to help other investors. For investors, part of their professional development is to learn from their mistakes. However, for homeowners, a home is a once-in-a-lifetime project and investment. Do you really want to go down the route of trial and error? Do you want to take that kind of risk for your life-changing investment?

For new build or 'knock down and rebuild' projects

If you plan to rebuild your home on your own land, a similar principle applies to avoid overcapitalising. You can get a valuation for the land itself and the valuation for the proposed new home plans from a certified valuer. Also, if you want to maximise the new build with an understanding of market-desirable configurations and pricing, a property consultant would give you the advice and analysis you need. This principle will help you set your budget to avoid overcapitalising.

Proper planning and research will avoid overcapitalising

The above principles help put your home building project at the right starting point. Without doing the necessary research and planning, you'll risk making emotional decisions instead of informed ones.

From my observation, homeowners who try to take on the mindset of a hybrid investor/ homeowner rarely arrive at a workable solution. On the contrary, it makes their decision-making process more complex and confusing. As we discussed earlier, a homeowner's mindset differs—or it should—from the investor's mindset. You need to be clear about your home's primary function and your goals and stick to them.

Setting your budget

Budget is another important element to look at to avoid overcapitalising. Many homeowners get stuck on this part of the project planning.

Who sets the budget?

We can't talk about overcapitalising without mentioning budget, because the two are closely related. Homeowners who worry about overcapitalising are usually those who are not sure about their budget too.

As an architect, I advise homeowners to take charge of their project budget. It is also advisable to work with a cost consultant to guide you in your project budgeting; architects are not the experts in cost. The architect will follow your direction and the cost consultant's advice to design accordingly.

A cost consultant is an independent consultant that homeowners engage as part of their team of experts. Their service gives you peace of mind so you won't go over budget and risk turning your dream home project into a nightmare and disappointment. A client who understands the cost consultant's role and the benefits of working with one said to me, 'Farinah, don't entertain those homeowners who do not want to engage cost consultants. Cost consultants are there to help homeowners, and they should engage them to their benefit.' That was the best advice I have ever received from a client!

This client used to work for a developer, and she understood that even developers, the building professionals, engage the services of cost consultants for their building projects. How much more does a homeowner who doesn't know the ins and outs of the industry need these services?

How do we set the budget?

One of the most common traps homeowners fall into is setting an unrealistic budget. They need to set their brief and requirements to match their budget. What I mean is: very often, homeowners set a higher expectation brief than their budget can accommodate.

What do I mean by brief? A brief is the homeowner's requirements, the scope of work, and their aspirations for the project. It can be detailed as to how many rooms, the size of each room, the function of the rooms, the style of the house, the finishes and materials used, the colour scheme, and so on.

Your brief needs to match your budget and needs to take into account the current market rates for construction. You must embrace this reality before getting too excited and jumping into the design process with your architect. The architect can only design in two ways: according to your budget or according to your brief.

If your brief doesn't match your budget, and the architect is asked to design according to your brief without knowing how much is in your budget, then the architect will most likely design something beyond your budget! This often happens when homeowners didn't set their budget before the design process or when homeowners are not transparent with the architect about their budget or what they are willing to spend.

Often homeowners misunderstand the architect's role and don't want to reveal their budget to the architect. But the architect is the homeowner's agent, looking out for your benefit. We don't sell architect-designed homes.

We provide a service. Our fee is only a fraction of your budget, as you can see from the Homeowner's Budget Planning template in the Bonus section.

Architects don't get to spend on your budget allowance—in fact, the opposite is true: we guide your spending by providing design that meets your needs and budget.

> **The architect can only design in two ways: according to your budget or according to your brief.**

Often clients ask, 'How much is it going to cost me to build such and such?' Unfortunately, that is the wrong question to ask an architect at the initial meeting before giving them your brief, requirements, and budget. The better approach to take is: 'This is my budget, and this is my brief and requirements. Do you think my budget is realistic for my brief?'

So I recommend homeowners create a brief before meeting with their architect. Have clarity on your goals and what you would like to achieve from your project.

It is also important to understand that once your budget is set, the architect's design and the brief need to be progressively adjusted and checked back to the budget. It is rarely a one-time exercise. Teamwork and trust need to be established to navigate this process.

Often, homeowners are caught up in the excitement of adding more to their Wishlist. They request the architect to design accordingly and then end up over budget. This is where the cost consultant's service will be valuable—to pull everyone's expectations back to the budget.

I have included the steps and template on how you can create your own brief. This will help you prioritise your needs and wants to align with your budget. I have also included a Homeowner's Budget Planning template to help you with the project budgeting. These templates are available for you to download in the Bonus section.

> **Not taking charge of your budget is like handing over your wallet for someone else to do the spending.**

I believe in homeowners taking charge of the budget. Your budget is like your wallet. Before you go out to do your shopping, you need to know how much you have, how much of it you plan to spend and what you need to buy. Not taking charge of your budget is like handing over your wallet for someone else to do the spending. Before you know it, you are over your budget!

The architect is not in charge of your budget or spending. Nobody is responsible for that role. *You* have full control and full ownership of your wallet. *You* decide how much you want to spend and what you want to spend it on. Your team of experts is there to give you advice, guidance, and input.

I trust that Section Two of this book, Industry Secrets, has helped you. Knowing the myths, truths, and industry secrets will open your eyes to what matters to you as a homeowner. I believe you will be empowered and equipped to make your own assessment and a decision that works for your unique situation.

We are moving to the final and most important section of the book, where we will look at topics such as trust, the architect's role, and industry changes. What are we going to do moving forward from here? What are you going to do as a homeowner, equipped with the knowledge you have gained so far? What can we expect from the industry?

Section Three
MOVING FORWARD

CHAPTER

INCREASING TRUST IN THE INDUSTRY

When I ask homeowners their number one concern in finding professionals to build their dream home, their answer is 'trust'.

Most homeowners have heard disaster stories of a dream home project turning into a nightmare—stories of project delay, unfinished work, defects not being rectified, budget overrun, a design that was too costly to build, a final product that was not as promised, and countless other horror stories.

Those stories shake homeowners' confidence and prevent some dream homes from being built. Many homeowners resort to settling for second best. Instead of enjoying a dream home that fits their needs like gloves on their hands, they adjust their lives to a 'good enough' home that they can find in the market. Rather than risk handing their dream to someone untrustworthy, they abandon it.

Those are the current situations that many homeowners experience. Sometimes professionals in the building industry betray your trust. As an architect serving in this industry for 15 years, I struggle with that reality too. In my own interactions, I have occasionally tasted the bitter fruits of what other professionals in this industry have done—and betrayed trust is not a pretty sight or a good feeling.

TRUST IS A KEY MISSING INGREDIENT IN THIS INDUSTRY

Have you been disappointed, cheated, and overcharged by someone who provided a service for your home improvement projects? They promised the sun and the moon, and you ended up with a lemon?

I have!

I know. I can't believe it either. After so many years working in the industry, I still fell through the cracks of being conned, right in my backyard, so to speak. But it happens, unfortunately.

Let me share the story of my blunder …

After a strong wind, a large tree fell in my parents' backyard. They told me they had found a tree lopper to remove it. Their friend had referred the tree lopper to them, and my parents were happy with his job.

A few months later, my parents wanted to widen one side of their driveway to allow easier access to the garage.

I drew a sketch to confirm what they had in mind, and planned to use the sketch to get three quotes. I found a tradesman referred by a relative. I met him and showed him the existing driveway. I showed him my sketch and explained what my parents wanted—all good. I got one quote and showed it to my parents.

Before I had completed getting the other two quotes, my parents told me they'd found a tradesman who could widen the driveway for them. And the best part, my dad said, was that his price was lower than the quote I got from the first tradesman. My parents told me they got their contact from the tree lopper.

So this concrete driveway tradie is the tree lopper's mate. I figured my parents were happy with the tree lopper's job, so his mate should be OK, right?

Well, that's where I got it wrong!

Since Dad had now found the guy he wanted, I planned to brief him on the existing driveway and show him the sketch of the proposed changes. This would be the exact same briefing I'd had with the first tradesman.

But as it turned out, my dad had made his own arrangement. He did some wheeling and dealing with this concrete driveway tradesman and short-circuited my process. The next thing I knew, the guy was in for the job! Dad made some payments; the tradie had done some work and planned to collect his last pay the following day.

When I heard that, my warning alarm went off. Questions raced through my head, in panic mode. *Wait a minute! I haven't even met this guy; I haven't shown him the sketch. Does he know what my parents want him to do? What kind of work has he done? What is he charging them? What is the payment plan?*

I had not seen his two days of work. He'd finish the job tomorrow and wanted the full payment? I didn't have peace about the whole situation.

I rushed back from my weekend break to check out what had been done to the driveway. Yep, sure enough: it was a botched job. I found out the full story from my parents—including the amount they'd been charged and the payment arrangements the tradesman had made with my dad. My heart sank.

What my parents thought was a bargain because of the cheaper quote turned out to be an expensive exercise! This person took advantage of an unsuspecting, trusting homeowner. He didn't do a decent job—far from it. It was a mess, and he actually damaged the existing driveway. It was so upsetting and frustrating.

I had to calm myself and put on my architect's hat. I told my dad that he couldn't wheel and deal like that. I let him know it wasn't wise to engage someone based solely on a cheaper quote without knowing whether they had the knowledge or skill to do the job.

I explained to my dad why I went through a process to get the quote. That is my process of qualifying the right person for the job. I would know through my conversation and briefing whether the person had the appropriate knowledge and understanding of the job.

We decided to stop this person from continuing the work because we didn't want him to do more damage.

I met him on the last day—the day he anticipated finishing his job. I told him he didn't need to complete the work. I pointed out the damage he had done and mentioned the GST (Goods and Services) charge he had misled my dad into paying. Australian GST is like VAT for European customers—the national sales tax that businesses collect on behalf of the government for the goods and services they provide. However, only businesses who are registered as GST businesses can charge GST. This guy was not registered.

It was stressful to resolve the situation and confront the tradesman's inappropriate conduct. However, I knew I had to confront him. It's the right thing to do as a professional—to speak for and defend unsuspecting victims from the industry's cowboys.

The building industry can be a treacherous place if you don't know how it works, and uninformed and unsuspecting homeowners like my parents are often targets and victims of the cowboys in the industry. What my dad thought was a cheaper price ended up costing him almost double; we needed to get someone else to fix the botched job and complete the work.

Scenarios similar to my parents' example can happen to any homeowner. They are common occurrences that we face in our work serving in this industry. Building and construction is a multi-billion-dollar industry in

Australia, and it is one of the country's economic engines. It attracts all kinds of people: the good, the bad, and the ugly.

What happened to my parents is just one example of what could go wrong in any home project. It was, however, a fraction of the cost compared with the amounts spent by people who are building a home. I urge homeowners to consider managing their projects carefully. Do not take chances and unnecessary risks for what you perceive as savings or bargains.

Those cowboy practices will not deliver value for your money. They'll give you shortcuts, headaches, and heartaches. You must work with people you can trust. Those who will give you independent advice and impartiality. Those who provide truthful information and empower you in making the right decision.

We pay independent consultants for the quality of the advice and their expertise. Their fees are not extra expenses. Consider their fees as part of your home project investment and insurance policy, something you need to budget for. They are there for your peace of mind and the security they bring for the success of your project.

As a Future Home owner, you can change the industry standard. If homeowners don't foster the ecosystem of poor practices, I believe we can weed cowboy operators out of the industry. No demand equals no supply needed.

My wish is for homeowners to enjoy transparency, honesty, and trust for the services they receive. I want the building and construction industry to produce better-quality homes and services, delivering better value for money. I believe it is possible, if all of us work together, to uphold a higher standard than we currently have. We need to work hand in hand, the professional service providers and the clients.

> **We pay independent consultants for the quality of the advice and their expertise. Their fees are not extra expenses.**

CHAPTER

DO I NEED AN ARCHITECT TO BUILD A HOUSE?

This is one of the questions most often asked by homeowners when they think of engaging an architect.

As I dig deeper into this question, I find other sentiments underlying it. Some of these are:

- 'An architect-designed house is more expensive to build.'
- 'Architect fees are expensive.'
- 'We just want a simple house; we don't need an architect's service.'
- 'We saw a floor plan that we like; we'll just use that plan and get someone to draw it for us.'
- 'We can use the building company that offers free design service.'

As a homeowner, you can relate to those views. You might have heard stories from friends who built their homes without an architect. Perhaps you read property investment books or articles that teach you how to DIY to save the professionals' fees.

Maybe you love to watch *The Block*, one of Australia's household reality TV series on renovations. You have some design flair. You can see how the judges pick the winner, because you have the same eye for good design as the judges.

You watch enough episodes of *The Block* to have an excellent collection of design ideas; you've learned how they manage their projects and what pitfalls to avoid. It seems achievable. You believe you can do the design yourself using computer drawing software or apps. In fact, you've watched some YouTube videos on how to use those software or apps, and it looked easy and fun.

With all this under your belt, you just need a builder to do the work and take care of the permit requirements for you. You'll save on the architect's fee.

What does an architect do, anyway? Do they just come up with those designs you see in glossy magazines? Those architect-designed houses always look like the dream home you have always wanted, but they also look out of this world, beyond your reach, and very expensive!

Those are stories I've collected over the years—the architect's image through the homeowner's lens. Are those pictures accurate?

WHAT MAKES A PERSON AN ARCHITECT?

In Australia and other parts of the world—like the USA, Canada, New Zealand, and the UK—apart from architects, other building practitioners such as draftspeople and building designers offer similar services. Other countries, like Singapore, recognise architects as the only building practitioner providing architectural services for all building projects.

In many countries, the title 'architect' is a protected term reflecting certain standards and requirements, and not all building practitioners can call themselves architects. In Australia, individuals who can use the title 'architect' need to complete a degree in architecture, gain several years of necessary professional experience, and register with the Board of Architects by passing an examination process.

After passing the registration process, then you can call yourself an architect. It is a rigorous process that takes eight years minimum.

I believe similar credentials and registration processes apply to other countries outside Australia—for example, Singapore, Malaysia, the USA, UK, and New Zealand.

Without being registered, we can't call ourselves an architect or practise as an architect, even if we have completed a university degree or master's degree in architecture and gained many years of experience in the industry afterwards.

The Board of Architects, in the states and territories where an architect practices, governs our registration. Architects are also bound by legislation such as the Architects Act 1991, Architects Regulations 2015, and the Architects Code of Professional Conduct within the states where we practice.

> **An architect's duty of care to the public carries almost the same weight as a doctor's. Building works can also cause injury, damage, and even loss of lives.**

WHAT'S THE BIG DEAL ABOUT USING AN ARCHITECT?

Architects' rigorous training and their code of conduct ensure that homeowners like yourself are protected by law and will receive quality service and care.

This provides security for homeowners, who can be assured that the registration's governing body and legislation will protect them. Architects need to demonstrate a high standard of integrity, competency, and impartiality to function and serve in our profession. In Australia, professional registration is another layer of protection for homeowners on top of the consumer protection law.

You might not realise this, but an architect's duty of care to the public carries almost the same weight as a doctor's. Building works can also cause injury, damage, and even loss of lives. Have you heard of the Lacrosse apartment fire in 2014 in Melbourne? Or the 2017 Grenfell Tower fire in London? These are examples of the execution of building construction gone wrong, and these errors don't only apply to high-rise buildings.

I heard the following true story from an architect who was brought up for inquiry. A homeowner tripped over the staircase in his home, designed by this architect. The owner wanted to make a case that the staircase's design caused him to trip, although that was not the real cause of the accident. Yep—as ridiculous as it sounds, that is the weight and responsibility of an architect's role.

> **Despite what many people think, homeowners do not pay architects for drawing up floor plans or designing fancy-looking houses.**

Here is another truth the general public might not know: as architects, our responsibility for our work doesn't stop after our careers finish. Our work and the buildings we designed can outlive our careers. As long as the building they designed still stands and functions, the architect's responsibility for their work stays with the building. That is why the industry requires us to carry insurance to cover our work, even after we retire! It is a lifetime commitment and calling. Becoming an architect is not something most of us take lightly.

It is the architect's responsibility to protect the public's safety and the welfare of the people we serve. Is there any wonder why architects charge their clients for advice, ideas, and design?

Even though the architects' responsibility and duty of care require similar standards to those of doctors and specialists, compared to a specialist's fee, an architect's fee doesn't come close. Hopefully, this chapter will give you an insight into an architect's role so you can make a better judgement the next time you ask yourself the question, 'Do I need an architect to build my Future Home?'

Despite what many people think, homeowners do not pay architects for drawing up floor plans or designing fancy-looking houses. Architects have wider roles, responsibilities, and value than that.

The level of transparency and impartiality that architects need to provide under the Architects Code of Professional Conduct is beyond what other building practitioners must do.

Some of the codes of conduct architects must follow include the duty to disclose paid referrals and endorsements of products, and to ensure there is no conflict of interest between client and architect during their provision of service. Those are high-transparency concerns that seldom exist in current commercial and marketing ethics.

Those checks and balances ensure that homeowners receive independent advice and service when working with an architect. The architect is free from any inducements or collusion from third parties. Ultimately, the homeowner can have peace of mind, knowing their architect is a trusted agent who represents their best interest with no hidden agendas or motives, no vested interest, and no conflict of interest. They offer only impartial and independent advice and service.

The fee you pay the architect is the only incentive the architect receives for your project. You pay the architect to be your trusted agent, adviser, and designer. Would you trust the advice you received if the architect did not have a duty to disclose any paid endorsement for a particular product or brand? How would you feel about the architect's recommendation if, out of the two options, the architect recommended the product or brand for which they were receiving incentives?

Have you heard stories about materials used in building projects that were not fit for their purpose and of inferior quality—where, after a few years, the problems surfaced? Whose role is it to advise you on material safety and value for your money?

Most architects emphasise the more permanent elements of your home—the design layout, the materials, and elements that are part of the building envelope. Having to replace those elements because of faulty or inferior quality is an expensive exercise. Plus, as discussed in Chapter Eleven, you might devalue your home if you make a mistake in designing a bad home layout.

Those are the big-ticket items you want to pay attention to when seeking an architect's advice and leverage on their expertise. Interior materials and equipment such as paint, lighting, and appliances are more forgiving. They can accommodate your design flair experiments and DIY adventures as they are easier and less costly to replace.

Here are some questions to consider if you are thinking of building your Future Home. Who takes care of the specification of the materials that go into your home? Who is your trusted adviser? Is it the salesperson who sells the material? Is it the builder who says they can provide you with alternative materials that are more cost-efficient than what the architect specified in the drawings?

Those are some unseen and unspoken roles of an architect. Their duty of disclosure and conflict of interest are important codes of conduct that ensure you receive trustworthy advice.

There are other building practitioners who charge clients for design fees and commissions on items they specify. Suppliers will offer a commission to the designer for items their client buys due to their recommendation. Not so with architects—we do not get any commission from the products we specify. We choose and specify products according to what is best for the project, is fit for the intended purpose, and benefits the client's safety and well-being.

Having served in this industry for many years, I've learned that peace of mind, security, and a sense of protection are important aspects that homeowners need to consider in their journey of building their dream home. Home is the biggest and sometimes the only investment most homeowners have.

You want to protect your asset and eliminate any risk of disasters and heartaches. You don't want to risk hundreds of thousands of dollars of your investment for the sake of a few perceived savings, such as the cost of receiving expert advice from an independent agent. You need to weigh the perceived savings over the risk you are exposing yourself to.

WHAT DOES AN ARCHITECT DO? WHY DON'T I SEE ARCHITECTS ON *THE BLOCK*?

If you've seen the TV series *The Block*, you haven't seen an architect's involvement in any of the projects. However, those aspiring renovators can achieve amazing results. Yes, I always wonder about that too! Where are the architect and the rest of the professional team of experts? Maybe that is the reason why *The Block* is a reality TV show?

In a real-life situation, architects are the guides, the advocates, the expert advisers, and the trusted agents to homeowners. Those are the essential roles of an architect.

The architect will guide and give expert advice to homeowners throughout the project, at every critical decision-making juncture. This ensures that homeowners can achieve their dreams and aspirations within the constraints of local and building regulations, their budget, the site conditions, and health and safety requirements.

The design stage—determining the homeowner's needs, aspirations, and dreams—is the creative part of an architect's job, the right-brain function. This is the more publicly understood role of an architect.

Prior to the design stage, the architect will do feasibility studies of your project, gathering information to do analytical work. This is like a doctor working towards a diagnosis. The architect will find out information about your site, the regulations, and your aspirations and goals. They will then advise you on the potential options you have for your site. This is the left-brain function of an architect's job description: the logical, analytical, and solution-based functionality.

As you progress further in the project, you will need to form a team of experts who specialise in particular areas of expertise. Depending on your project, the architect will advise and guide you on what additional experts you need in your team.

The architect will lead your team of experts and coordinate their work to form one unified set of drawings, documents, and specifications for your project. This set of drawings and documents is what we call construction drawings. This is the blueprint for the builder to construct your home.

The blueprint construction drawings and documents contain the details of all the elements and materials that make up your home; they are like your home's DNA. The blueprint shows the builder how to put all the elements together, including the internal and the external skin of your home—the things you can see and the things you can't, from the insulation behind the walls to details like your paint colours, the benchtop materials, the pattern and colours of the tiles, and so on.

This blueprint needs to comply with all the regulations and the building code, as confirmed by a building surveyor who issues the building permit. That permit allows the builder to start the construction works.

The public also often misunderstands this process of getting permits. Some homeowners believe the builder helps them get the building permit, but the truth is that the permit is issued based on a set of drawings and specifications put together by the architect, including those done by the rest of the team of experts/consultants.

As you can appreciate, building a home is a complex, concerted, and intricate process of teamwork. That is just a glimpse of the overall process. I won't bore you with the details in this book. When you work with an architect, the architect will explain the full process specific to your project.

WHO CHOOSES THE BUILDER?

As the homeowner, you do the choosing, but the architect can help you with the qualifying process so you can arrive at an informed decision.

Remember the story from the previous chapter about my parents' experience with their concrete driveway? To prevent blunders like that, I go through what I call a qualification process. I meet up with the different tradespeople, explaining the existing condition and the desired new work. That process gives me insight into whether the person has the knowledge and skill required to do the work. That is a similar picture of what an architect will do to help you shortlist suitably qualified builders for your project.

I'VE WORKED WITH A BUILDER BEFORE; WHY DO I NEED AN ARCHITECT FOR THE CONSTRUCTION STAGE?

You might be wondering why you need an architect once the plans are drawn up and the builder chosen. You might think it's unnecessary. But consider this. The builder's role is to construct your home according to the construction blueprint. Do you have a third party who can verify whether the builder follows the blueprint's design intent? How will you know whether the builder builds according to the drawing's specifications? What checks and balances do you have planned?

Do you know whether the builder's claim for payment is a true reflection of the amount of work done? What will you do if the builder says the project will be delayed?

It might be a surprise to you, but the architect's role is to be the homeowner's advocate, trusted agent, and an independent third party during the construction stage. Anyone who has managed building and construction projects, no matter how small—like my parents' driveway—or large—like a home, will testify that it is stressful. Construction stage is time sensitive, fast paced, and high risk.

Everything is live and in motion; it is no longer drawings on paper. Any errors can be very costly at this stage.

The story of my parents' driveway is a perfect example of what can happen if homeowners do not have an architect to help them navigate the construction stage. The cowboys in the industry, if you happen to meet them, are likely to take unsuspecting and uninformed homeowners for a ride.

Having someone you can trust gives you peace of mind and levels the playing field. Homeowners who forgo an architect's help during construction also forgo their right to have representation during this most complicated and critical stage of the project. It is like someone who goes to a court hearing as a lay person, without an advocate to defend them, facing an opponent who is a well-versed lawyer.

I've heard many sad stories of homeowners with abandoned projects, people making upfront payments to a builder who ran off with their money or engaging a professional who was not registered or insured, and clients who suffered imbalanced contract terms and conditions, delays in completion time, and many other complications and disasters.

Most of the disaster stories I hear are the result of homeowners trying to navigate the construction stage independently, without the help of a professional.

Imagine the builder came to you in the middle of the construction phase, asking about the architect's drawings or the design intent, or wanting clarification on the drawings. The builder uses industry terms and jargon you can't understand and expects you to make choices and decisions in, say, 48 hours. Time is critical at this stage, and you could cause a delay on the project, which means the builder could charge you extra if you can't come up with a good solution or answer within the critical timeframe. What would you do?

Plus, once you make your decision, it'll be set in concrete—I mean this literally and not just figuratively! Sure, you can change your mind after that, but it will cost you for extra material, labour, and time plus the builder's profit margin, as agreed in the contract.

Even to an architect—a professional, familiar with how the industry works—this stage is the most complicated. It can be stressful and consumes a lot of energy, time, and effort.

Many articles written by property investors give advice and tips on navigating this stage. Interestingly, many of the authors wrote those articles based on their mistakes. If those investors, who supposedly know the industry, still make mistakes that cost them time and money, I wouldn't recommend homeowners taking the same risk for the biggest and most important asset in their lives. It's not worth the risks and heartache, is it?

The building and construction industry is unfortunately not as straightforward as many people think or say. It is not the way the reality television show portrays it. I have heard of homeowners losing their life's savings, relationship breakdowns, and other sad stories—all because they perceive they'll save money by not hiring a professional. But the professional's fee is your insurance policy; you need to budget for it. It is not an extra expense. Trying to manage without a professional is like owning a car without buying car insurance: not a wise move.

> **Construction stage is time sensitive, fast paced, and high risk.**

In this industry, I learned that no matter what you do, these three elements will always balance themselves out—time, quality, and cost.

I hear of homeowners who will go all out to save on professionals' fees by attempting a DIY job or engaging part-time service from the professionals. At the outset, it looks like they are saving on cost. However, the DIY and trial-and-error effort will delay their project; that's time.

And guess what else is affected by a delay in their project? It goes back to cost! Time costs money. When the project is delayed, homeowners pay rent for longer than they'd anticipated, an extra expense beyond the original budget. Also, the builder has a contracted completion timeline. If that timeline is delayed, the extended project time will affect the builder's project schedules, manpower and finances, which may trigger an extra claim from the builder, called variations, if the homeowner causes the delay. That's another extra cost to homeowners.

So, what is the final saving? Are there, in fact, any savings at all from not engaging the professionals?

This story reminds me of driving around town to look for a petrol station that has a better price. How much do we save? A few cents per litre or a few dollars in total? What is the cost for us going that extra mile? Another litre of petrol, which amounts to the 'saving' we make? And how much time have we wasted? How does that realisation make you feel?

MY PERSONAL STORY

Here's my personal story of the architect's role during the construction stage.

A few years ago, I worked on a community building project as an architectural graduate in one of the architect firms in Melbourne, Australia. It was a sizeable project—a second-storey extension to an existing community building—worth a few million dollars.

The client's task force assigned one of their board members to follow the project's progress and attend all the site meetings. It was a complex project for many reasons, including the size of the extension and the nature of the work. Like most renovation projects, it had many unknowns.

The client's board member closely followed what we needed to resolve during the 12-month construction stage. He was in the loop for every communication the architect's team had with the builder, all the paperwork, and the on-site resolutions. Additionally, the site meetings sometimes turned into interesting episodes of high tension between the architect's team and the builder's team. I was glad to be the lady in those meetings. At least the gents restrained themselves a bit while I was in their presence—I probably prevented a few fist-fights just by being in the room. No kidding!

During the construction stage, architects represent their client to ensure that the builder carries out the work per the drawings and written specifications; essentially, these are the contract documents. Architects also administer the progress claims from the builder. In this role, the architect acts as a certifier, an independent assessor between the two parties of the contract: the client and the builder. The architect's role is to check that the claims are true regarding the work that has been done and to certify the progress claim for the client to pay the builder.

Architects must do a balancing act to remain fair and independent certifiers. During the construction stage, especially at that scale, budget and time are crucial, and there is often tension between the client and the builder. As architects, we can be like the meat in the sandwich, and ours is not a straightforward job!

In this instance, the rewarding part came at the end of the project, when everyone saw the drawings come alive. All parties felt joy and satisfaction. Everyone's blood pressure went back to normal. No rude or shocking emails to attend to. No late nights thinking through the solutions for the builder to work on-site. No early morning phone calls from the site manager on what went wrong. It was celebration time for the team and the client!

Here is another good ending to the story. Do you remember the board member who had been following the architect's team throughout the project? At the end of the project, he said, 'Now I understand how much work and stress architects have to go through. Thank you for your hard work.' I believe it was an eye-opener for the board member; following the full process gave him the awareness to fully appreciate the scope of an architect's role during the construction stage.

You might say this story represents a much bigger project than the average home project. That is true. But do you know that the steps and the process for any construction work are very much the same? A smaller project like a house goes through the same process as a big community building in order to get from a concept to a life-size home or building.

Building a home, just like any other significant project, requires teamwork and cooperation from everyone involved. It's important to have the client, architect, builder, and other consultants work together to achieve a great outcome. Homeowners must surround themselves with a team of experts to help them turn their dreams into reality.

WE JUST WANT A SIMPLE HOUSE; WE DON'T NEED AN ARCHITECT

There's a secret I would like to share.

As homeowners, you might like to take advantage of this secret when choosing your building practitioners. Being an architect and interacting with my peers, I realise architects do not think and design in two-dimensional form. An architect's mind and the ways in which we process information can be very complex. It reminds me of a book titled *Men Are Like Waffles, Women Are Like Spaghetti*.[28] An architect's brain processing can be like spaghetti, everything connected to everything else.

Architects are trained to think in three-dimensional form, which means we see your house floor plans as spaces and rooms rather than as flat two-dimensional drawings. It's second nature for us to think that way because of our many years of training. If that surprises you, you're welcome to check this fact with your architect the next time you see them!

How would that three-dimensional way of thinking make any difference to you as a homeowner? Well, when architects think in this way, they help you create beautiful spaces you love to be in—spaces with a sense of place rather than just rooms. Your home will have a heart and a soul and evoke your senses and feelings. That is the magic difference!

CHAPTER THIRTEEN: DO I NEED AN ARCHITECT TO BUILD A HOUSE?

Have you ever been to a place and felt wonderful just by being there? It can look like a simple room—not necessarily big or filled with glamorous decorations, but you can just sense the magic in there. Maybe it's the way the light shines through the room, or perhaps the window is perfectly positioned. That's the magic an architect can help you create for your dream home.

I've met homeowners who've told me they didn't hire an architect for their home project. They'd done their own research on the home layout and the type of homes they like. They'd watched a lot of episodes of *Grand Designs Australia*, and they were confident in developing the house layout themselves.

They also ventured into using computer software to draw the house plan themselves. I admire those homeowners who are so passionate and committed to their projects. However, there are a couple of misconceptions that leave gaps in their mindsets:

- Misconception 1: architects design floor plans.
- Misconception 2: an architect's expertise is in drawing plans using a computer—some might say that architects just draw pretty pictures.

Here is another secret I'll share with you, but only if you promise not to question your architect about it: generally, in an architect's office, if the grand design ideas come from the senior architect untrained in computer drawing software, guess how those designs will be presented? Believe it or not, they usually come in the form of sketches on paper or scribbles on napkins, sometimes even with coffee stains. Guess who does the computer drawing? It's the junior staff in the office!

My point is that anyone tech-savvy can draw a set of floor plans using software. It is the idea, the concept, the creation of a space that makes the architect's service valuable and worthwhile.

The beautiful drawings of floor plans and three-dimensional images present the ideas, which is an important part of the process. However, that is not why you hire an architect. Anyone can experiment with drawing up a floor plan with computer software, and anyone can come up with a floor plan with the number of rooms you need, of the sizes you want. The main benefit for homeowners hiring an architect is that architects are trained to design and process information beyond those obvious requirements.

Architects utilise more information than you tell us during our conversation. We listen to the stories you tell about how your family likes to get together on Friday nights for a movie or how you like to go outside and look at the stars on a clear cloudless night. By combining all that seemingly unrelated information with your thoughts on how many and what types of rooms you want, we find the right connections, process them, and turn them into a created space that brings joy to you. Yes, our brains are like spaghetti! But we also have the means of sorting that spaghetti into an appealing dish.

We also process the obvious information and research that we need in terms of the regulation requirements, the buildability and feasibility, the site conditions of your particular plot of land, the different materials that meet the standard, the budget, coordination with the other consultants, and so on.

I hope by now you have a better understanding of an architect's role, so you can make the most of the architect's skill and expertise to add value to your project and your life.

I have a perfect story to illustrate how an architect's brain works. A couple came to me to do a design concept of their home. They gave me their requirements of the rooms they needed, and they also showed me a concept done by another building practitioner who is not an architect. They wanted to know the difference between my service as an architect and the other building practitioner's service. Fair enough!

When I showed them the concept I had done, their main response was that I'd created a design that met the differing needs of each of them. They didn't expect that I would take the extra information I gathered during our conversations—the different things each person liked—and include that in the design. I had included surprise elements highlighting a sense of space that wasn't reflected in the other building practitioner's design.

CHAPTER THIRTEEN: DO I NEED AN ARCHITECT TO BUILD A HOUSE?

I believe homeowners need to look at those differentiations between architects and other building practitioners. Decide what is important to you, your family, and your project. Why do you want to hire an architect? What is the value you are looking for from the architect's experience and skill set?

Your home—especially your Future Home—is for long-term future living. Is it worth hiring the right professional for the biggest investment in your life? Or would you rather save on professionals' fees in exchange for the risk of disappointment and regrets?

Let's now look at one of the questions we raised at the start of this chapter.

IS AN ARCHITECT-DESIGNED HOME MORE EXPENSIVE TO BUILD?

I trust that by now you understand the role of the architect and the meanings of overcapitalisation and budget. Understanding these matters hopefully answers the question above. No, an architect-designed home is not more expensive to build.

Why? Because the architect designs your home according to your budget and your needs, as we discussed in Chapter Eleven. It is your budget and the construction market rate that determines the cost of building your home. Architects don't design homes to sell. The 'brand' of 'architect-designed home', if you want to look at it that way, is not more expensive than cookie-cutter homes built in volume or spec homes.

However, there is good news about the value of an architect-designed home. Recent research by the University of Melbourne and ArchiTeam in Australia found that houses with renovations designed by small-practice architects outperform non-architect-designed houses. The study confirms that small-practice architect-designed renovation homes in Melbourne improve capital gains by 1.2% per annum. It also found that for every $1 spent on architectural fees, $11.40 is gained in capital appreciation over 10 years.[29]

> **It is your budget and the construction market rate that determines the cost of building your home. Architects don't design homes to sell.**

I believe this research reiterates the value of investing in an architect-designed home and architect fees.

Last but not least, this is a question raised by one of the editors of this book. A good question, which I realised is not simple to answer!

WHERE CAN I FIND AN ARCHITECT'S SERVICE?

Interestingly, architects' services are not widely advertised. Additionally, architects generally aren't great marketers—perhaps because we learned little about the business side of architecture in our training. Instead, we focused on developing our professional skills and craft.

In the history of architecture as a profession, in the 1900s it was considered unprofessional for architects to advertise their services. However, the profession has changed over the decades. An architect's service, like any other professional service, is part of the free-market economy, determined by consumer supply and demand.

In my observation as a practising architect, sadly, there are not enough avenues that connect architects with everyday homeowners or the general public. That may be why many homeowners don't think an architect's service is necessary or even valuable.

Public perceptions that architects are only for luxury homes or the rich and famous do not help break these misconceptions of everyday homeowners. And added to the misconception is the wealth of TV and media information that teaches homeowners that self-help and DIY reduce costs.

In saying all that, more homeowners come to architects through referral than any other way. Some architects advertise their services through online media such as online magazines, LinkedIn, other social media, Google, and so on.

Two years before writing this book, I found myself frustrated with the lack of public awareness of architects' contribution to the housing industry. There seemed to be a barrier between architects and the general public. Yet everyday homeowners would benefit from the architect's service if we can bridge this gap.

This realisation prompted me to write this book—I wanted to share my knowledge and understanding of the housing market from an architect's perspective to the public, to bridge that gap that separates us.

You can also find an architect through reading materials, books, blogs, magazines, and articles written by architects or about the architect's projects. Another likely source for finding an architect's services is through related professions in the building and construction industry—property planning experts, real estate agents, builders, and other building consultants.

Your state's architects' registration board is the safest place to find registered architects in your area. When you find an architect's name on the registration board, you are assured that the person is a registered architect with the required credentials, code of conduct, and necessary insurances.

The next step is to find out how compatible and comfortable you are with the architect's experience, work ethics, and synergy. It is important that you find someone you can trust, communicate with, and connect well with, because you will be working with them for the long term. A typical home project spans 18 months to two years, from design to completion of construction. It is a long-term working relationship.

I trust this chapter has enlightened you to make wise choices and informed decisions on whether you need an architect to build your home.

You might still say, 'I don't need an architect to build my house'. That is well and good. If you're reading this now and that is still your belief, you at least have a full picture and understanding of your decision. My role is to lay out the truth for you to consider, so you can make an informed decision that works for your family's situation.

As an architect, it is a joy to serve clients who appreciate and value my gift to meet their needs. We all have unique gifts and talents. I too receive services from others who use their gifts to supply my needs in areas where I am not as gifted as them. This book in your hand is the result of that! I surround myself with a team of experts to make this book a success and a valuable gift to you as the reader. My team of experts consists of editors, book cover designer, book formatter, proofreader, and a writing coach. Yes, I do practice what I advise!

I believe using our gifts and talents to benefit others brings joy to both the giver and the receiver of the gift. It is not just a transactional exchange but a relational exchange. It makes the world a better place to live in. You usually can spot those who love what they do by how they make you feel when they provide the service for you. They energize you and make you feel special!

Can you believe we have travelled so far in this book? You are getting to know the ins and outs of what it takes to build a home, how the industry works, what options and choices are available to you to build a future-proof home. Are you ready for the last chapter? It's going to be a lookout point and a launching pad for you!

CHAPTER 14

INDUSTRY CHANGE

Congratulations on hanging on till the last chapter!

I hope you have received tons of value, new insights, and practical knowledge from reading this book so far. I trust this chapter will be the most important one for you as a homeowner, because this is where you will make important decisions moving forward.

Having served in this industry for 15 years, I've learned a lot about how it works, the mindset of its professionals, and the public's sentiments about it.

I personally believe the industry has a lot more room for improvement and change. Homeowners have been let down, and the industry has broken their trust in the past. Past failures continue and create current conditions.

Many homeowners prefer to trust in what they can do themselves rather than working with the professionals in the industry. It is hard for people to know who they can trust to do the job and who has their best interests at heart. I understand that to be true for many homeowners who share their thoughts with me. However, it should not be that way.

I believe in providing homeowners with honest, unbiased information. In doing so, I empower you to make your own decision to move in a direction that will benefit you, your family, and future generations. It will also change the industry for the better as a result. We will produce better products and weed out the cowboys.

Together, we will prevent unscrupulous people in the industry from taking advantage of unsuspecting homeowners and turning them into casualties. Homeowners who are lured by rock-bottom prices that come with a hidden price tag are often devastated.

I believe with the right education, information, and perspective, homeowners will create a change in the demand for a different type of home: a Future Home—a home that adapts to the different phases of your life. A home that truly serves your needs and well-being.

Your voice will cause the industry to respond to your needs. It will change the way the industry innovates. We will produce better homes that genuinely add value and enhance everyone's lives, even giving opportunity and hope to the next generation of homeowners.

Home is one of the biggest investments most people make in their lives, and homeowners deserve a better product than the industry has given them so far.

Since the global pandemic, I believe homeowners worldwide are awakening to the new reality of how important a home is to themselves and their families. This new awareness is timely preparation for homeowners, moving forward, to examine how they currently live and how they want to live in the future.

Building your Future Home is a long-term investment. I hope what you've read here has helped you change your priorities and offered a new perspective on the importance of building Future Home.

You will be more intentional in investing in things that matter—quality versus quantity. You understand the importance of investing in long-lasting features that provide comfort and enhance your health and well-being: features that save on running costs, rather than being mere bright shiny objects; features that provide flexibility and adaptability rather than being fixed and rigid; features that are intended for long-term rather than short-term use.

As informed homeowners, you have the power to change the industry and its trends. The industry responds to supply and demand; when it sees that homeowners demand better homes, it will have to respond with the supply the market demands.

It is no longer the case that industry professionals, investors, and realtors can talk you into what makes a wonderful home. It is your turn to realign their mindsets to your needs, to let them know what is important to you, what you value about a home, and what type of home you and your family would like to live in.

It is time to change the way we build our homes. Our society has changed at a greater speed than ever before. Family dynamics, socioeconomic issues, employment, and the rising costs of living, land and property are factors that affect every one of us. You and your family are part of these dynamics and this ecosystem.

The demand and supply of homes affects homeowners. Currently, the supply of houses in the market does not meet the needs of many homeowners—and I'm not referring solely to quantity. I believe the solution does not arise from just building more houses, units, and apartments of the same quality.

We need to build better—better quality and with a better understanding of homeowners' needs.

It's a matter of quality versus quantity. Quantity can be scaled up easily once we have the right product and the right quality.

I've heard more stories in recent years from homeowners who couldn't find suitable homes in the current market. Homeowners who understand the importance of looking at their homes as long-term investments and a legacy for the next generation. They are looking for a home that adapts to the different phases of their lives—a Future Home for future living.

Baby boomers want to move out of their family home to their growing-old home. A home with livable features—the Future Home features that we discussed in Chapter Seven. They want homes that can comfortably accommodate their future movement and physical restrictions.

Families with younger children want to live in comfortable, lower-maintenance homes that are less costly to run. Homes for their family to grow in until the children are ready to move out. Homes where they build family history, memories, and legacy.

Some homeowners want to leave a legacy for the next generation by maximising the use of their home to be adaptable to changes in their lives. They want to limit the number of times they move to save costs and unfavourable trading of assets.

Other homeowners hold their family values and traditions dear. They desire to pass them on to the next generation through multigenerational living, enhancing the value of caring and sharing to close the generational gaps.

And then there are homeowners who put their priority on quality rather than quantity. They prefer to adopt compact living rather than competing with the Joneses and their McMansion homes. They know that the 'less is more' lifestyle saves on construction costs, invests in quality materials and helps the environment by creating less waste.

Locally in Australia and globally in the world, those are the cries from homeowners.

You might not realise it, but the next generation of homeowners is coming sooner than you expect. If you are parents of the millennial generation, you will have heard their cries. They are future homeowners; however, most of them have given up the idea and hope of home ownership. They might be forced to adopt the idea of renting—for a lifetime. Is this a legacy we want to leave to the next generation?

I would like to share one more story, which I find very unsettling. This is one of those stories that kept me awake those nights at the start of my book-writing journey.

A few years ago, I received a phone call one day and heard this: 'Farinah, Ben has to move out of his rented house. His landlord wants to take back the house. He doesn't have a place to stay. Do you know anyone who can help him?' I was shocked and speechless. I couldn't believe what I heard.

Ben had been renting for many years. He works as an independent contractor, providing service to companies and organisations. Unfortunately, the economic slowdown affected his ability to get enough workflow, which reduced his income. Coupled with the landlord wanting to take back the home he had rented for so long, this pushed Ben out of his home. Suddenly, he found himself in a precarious position where he couldn't find an affordable rental home in the private market.

Everything changed in Ben's life after that incident. For a few months, he seemed to live like a homeless person. Thankfully, he eventually found a home through a government social housing programme, after many months of uncertainty and agony.

Ben's situation reflected the unnerving reality of the housing situation in Australia and other parts of the world. I didn't realise how challenging housing in Australia had become until that incident. Homelessness can affect anyone in society, even the middle class, because of two factors: job stability and housing affordability.

That incident was another pivotal moment that inspired me to find ways to educate homeowners on how to use their homes as long-term investments. It is also the reason I was compelled to write this book about Future Home.

When homeowners invest in their homes for long-term use, they save on the costs of moving, buying and selling, and moving in and out of the housing market. You can use those savings for building a better-quality home that meets your needs throughout the changes in your life. You invest in long-term use and planning.

> **As you adopt the idea of Future Home, you also help the future generations of your family. You help them gain a home that they too can enjoy when you leave your legacy.**

You will also be able to leverage the capital growth if you invest for the long term. Plus, you get to enjoy the use of a home that meets your needs. Even if you decide to sell your home at a later stage, the capital growth of the property and the land will likely pay back the cost of building your Future Home. Planning—financial planning and project planning—is the key.

The future trend of home ownership is another topic about which I'm concerned. According to the 2016 Census, the home ownership rate in Australia is 67%. This rate has seen a continuous downward trend since the mid-1960s.[30]

A lower rate of home ownership gives rise to a higher risk of homelessness. The millennial generation and beyond are the most vulnerable if we do not change the way we build our homes. The rising cost of housing bumps people in this age bracket into a tenancy lifestyle—this can be a risk factor for homelessness, as in the case of what I saw happen to Ben.

I understand that homelessness is a complex issue in our modern society. There are many causes, and there is no one solution or one industry that can fix this issue. Many facets are involved, and different industries need to work together to provide ways to prevent and manage the current global housing crisis.

CHAPTER FOURTEEN: INDUSTRY CHANGE

I believe it takes one willing person to change history. One person's effort matters and makes a difference to the collective whole. Sometimes, it takes just one person to create the domino effect that inspires others and gathers the momentum for change. Will you be that one homeowner that creates the change?

What one homeowner does to change the culture and trend of the industry makes a difference. We have gone through the cycle, with the industry producing homes they project will meet homeowners' needs and demands. Australia's 'poster child' home is a four-bedroom family home, and these are the homes the industry has been building for many decades.

But recent changes in our society, family units, socioeconomic issues, and lifestyle have awakened many homeowners to realise that we need something different. We need various kinds of homes for homeowners in different seasons of their lives, with different needs, goals, and aspirations.

As informed homeowners or aspiring homeowners, I trust you will have a fresh perspective and purpose on the type of Future Home you will build. What features will you invest in? What is the investment that matters to you and your family?

As you adopt the idea of Future Home, you also help the future generations of your family. You help them gain a home that they too can enjoy when you leave your legacy. Even if they rebuild a new home on the existing land you leave them, they will have gained savings on the cost of buying the land, which, as we have learned, is a limited resource that will go up in value in the future.

My wish is that you will make the right decision by adopting Future Home principles and build or renovate a home that's built to last, for you, your family, and the generations to come. You have the power to make the difference and be the difference!

Thank you for investing your time in educating and equipping yourself by reading this book. I trust you'll find the best solution, working with your team of experts in building your Future Home.

ABOUT THE AUTHOR— FARINAH HUSODO

I believe in living life to the fullest, following my passions and dreams, and using my gifts and talents to serve others and impact their lives.

My parents, siblings, and I migrated from Indonesia to Melbourne, Australia, when I was a teenager. Following my parents' dream of giving us children a better quality of life and education, we started a new life in Australia.

I arrived in Australia with almost zero English language skills. The first few months of school were terrifying. I came home understanding only 30% of what the teachers taught or said, except for the subject of maths.

After a period of adjustment, I enjoyed my schooling years. I adapted well to the new culture, people, and place. I was privileged to be later accepted to the school of architecture at the University of Melbourne, and received my architecture degree. I am grateful for the life I've lived and the education I've received.

I love architecture because it combines art and science, beauty and functionality. Since childhood, I have enjoyed creative works and had a curious mind; I always wanted to know how things fit together and how they function best. Architecture fits well with my natural inclinations.

My architecture principle is creating a simple, beautiful space, functioning to its original design intent for the joy of its users. I believe we can enjoy both beauty and function in our homes, just as nature around us blends those two elements. Beauty brings pleasure to our souls, and function helps us live a purposeful life.

After I graduated, I worked and lived overseas in Singapore. It was my first adventure away from home, in yet another foreign country. This time, English was not the problem, but Mandarin Chinese and the local dialect were. Thankfully, I got away with speaking mainly English, as most Singaporeans are multilingual. However, during my time in Singapore, I did manage to pick up simple conversational Mandarin Chinese and the local dialect.

I worked as an architectural graduate for a few years in Singapore, which enriched my life experience, skills, and appreciation for diverse cultures and people. Working in Singapore also allowed me to travel to other nearby countries, which further strengthened my understanding of the importance of people in architecture and the built environment. Architecture is not just about buildings or places, but about the people and cultures that make the place.

I appreciated the opportunity to return to Melbourne, Australia, after my adventure in Singapore. I have served in the building and construction industry for 15 years in Singapore and Australia on a diverse range of projects—such as detached houses, resorts, multi-residential developments, commercial fit-outs, education and childcare centres, and community buildings.

I am a registered architect practising in Victoria, Australia, and I founded an architecture practice, Studio M514. This book reflects my passion for helping homeowners build their Future Home—a home to meet their current and future needs, an adaptable home for the different phases of their lives.

I look forward to serving as an architect in the building and construction industry as well as the next adventure that life brings me.

CHAPTER FOURTEEN: INDUSTRY CHANGE

The following is one of my favourite quotes:

Twenty years from now you will be more disappointed by the things that you didn't do than by the ones you did do. So throw off the bowlines.

*Sail away from the safe harbor.
Catch the trade winds in your sails.*

Explore. Dream. Discover.

H. JACKSON BROWN JR., *P.S. I LOVE YOU* (1991)

You can connect with me at
studiom514.com.au
Facebook page **@studiom514**

ACKNOWLEDGMENTS

This, being my first book, is one of the most challenging projects I have ever attempted. I didn't realise that writing a book is very much like building a home or any other building project. Now I can appreciate the effort and work that goes into a book!

In saying all that, I am glad I ventured and stumbled into this world. I met wonderful and talented people who became part of this book's team of experts. Their input and service made this book a reality and a worthy resource for you, the readers and Future Home owners. It truly is a team effort!

Thank you to my team of experts!

Writing coach
Scott Allan, bestselling author and coach from the Self-Publishing School. (https://self-publishingschool.com)

Your timely guidance to answer all my questions gave me the assurance and peace of mind that I had a trusted guide to take me to the finishing line.

Editors and proofreader
I'd be lost without words to express my thoughts without your service and input.

- *Susan Michaud* (https://thesageproofreader.com)

  I appreciate your guidance, sharp eyes and attention to detail. Your help with the first copy edit of the manuscript and arranging everything in consistent order was invaluable.

- *Amy Pattee Colvin* (https://www.amycolvinwordsmith.com)

  Your editorial assessment was so helpful to set me on the right track from the start. Your ideas and suggestions, coming from across the globe, helped me consider readers from different parts of the world. You expanded my horizon and my heart to serve a bigger audience!

- *Alison Birch* (https://rewritten.uk)

  Your copy editing and proofreading tightened up all the loose ends and made the manuscript succinct and sharp. You polished my writing to shine!

There are others in the team who laboured with me throughout the journey with their support, encouragement and caring thoughts, believing in the mission and message I wished to share in this book.

Thank you to my book journey supporters, writing buddy and family!

Book journey supporters
Stephen, Julien, Judy, Fiona, Linda, Cheryl and other individuals who prefer to remain anonymous: we've made it! Many times, I felt lost amid mountains of decisions and unexpected twists and turns along the journey; your one-line messages, words of encouragement and thoughts have been my strength to go on and persevere. A big heartfelt thank you!

My writing buddy
Lidia, thank you for your encouragement and the time we spend discussing our books and keeping each other accountable. Let's go, buddy!

My family
Thank you for believing in me, accepting my gifts and talents and giving me the freedom to pursue my passion and dreams.

Thank you, Mum and Dad, for your sacrifice in taking a brave venture to start a new life for our family; you gifted us with education and a new home in the great south land, Australia.

Thank you, my brother and sisters, you are always in my heart. I love that you are all uniquely gifted in your own wonderful ways. You add beautiful colours to my life!

REFERENCES

Chapter One

1 Kusher, C. (2019). *Length of home ownership continues to rise* [online]. Available at: https://www.corelogic.com.au/news/length-home-ownership-continues-rise [Accessed 29 Jan. 2021].

Chapter Five

2 CommSec (2019). *Australian houses shrink: Smallest in 17 years* [online]. Available at: https://www.commbank.com.au/content/dam/caas/newsroom/docs/MDBiggest191111_non.pdf [Accessed 29 Jan. 2021].

3 Rider Levett Bucknall (2020). *Australia Report – COVID-19 Edition, Second Quarter 2020* [online]. Available at: https://s28259.pcdn.co/wp-content/uploads/2020/06/RLB-Australia-Report_Q2_2020.pdf [Accessed 29 Jan. 2021], p.6.

4 Singapore Housing & Development Board (2020). *Types of flats* [online]. Available at: https://www.hdb.gov.sg/cs/infoweb/residential/buying-a-flat/new/types-of-flats [Accessed 29 Jan. 2021].

5 ICC (2017). *2018 International Resident Code* [online]. Available at: https://codes.iccsafe.org/content/IRC2018/appendix-q-tiny-houses [Accessed 29 Jan. 2021].

6 Biophilia and building design. (n.d.). Available at: https://www.designingbuildings.co.uk/wiki/Biophilia_and_building_design [Accessed 4 Jul. 2021].

Chapter Six

7 Sinek, S. (2011). *Start with Why: How Great Leaders Inspire Everyone to Take Action*. London: Portfolio Penguin, p. 40.

8 Wikipedia (2021). *Millennials* [online]. Available at: https://en.wikipedia.org/wiki/Millennials [Accessed 30 Jan. 2021].

9 Pew Research Center (2012). *Who are the boomerang kids?* [online]. Available at: https://www.pewsocialtrends.org/2012/03/15/who-are-the-boomerang-kids [Accessed 30 Jan. 2021].

10 Cohn, D.V. and Passel, J.S. (2018). *Record 64 million Americans live in multigenerational households* [online]. Available at: https://www.pewresearch.org/fact-tank/2018/04/05/a-record-64-million-americans-live-in-multigenerational-households [Accessed 29 Jan. 2021].

11 Liu, D. (2020). *Moving back in: The rise of multigenerational households* [online]. Available at: https://www.be.unsw.edu.au/news/moving-back-rise-multigenerational-households [Accessed 5 Feb. 2021].

12 Cini, L.M. (2017). *Hive: the simple guide to multigenerational living: how our family makes it work*. Bloomington, IN: iUniverse.

13 Wikipedia (2020). *Fujian tulou* [online]. Available at: https://en.wikipedia.org/wiki/Fujian_tulou [Accessed 30 Jan. 2021].

Chapter Seven

14 Australian Bureau of Statistics (2020). *Life tables, 2017–2019* [online]. Available at: https://www.abs.gov.au/statistics/people/population/life-tables/2017-2019 [Accessed 29 Jan. 2021].

15 Livable Housing Australia (2017). *Livable Housing Design Guidelines*. 4th ed. [online]. Available at: http://www.livablehousingaustralia.org.au/library/SLLHA_GuidelinesJuly2017FINAL4.pdf [Accessed 30 Jan. 2021].

Chapter Eight

16 Wikipedia (2021). *Room temperature* [online]. Available at: https://en.wikipedia.org/wiki/Room_temperature [Accessed 30 Jan. 2021].

17 Milne, G., Reardon, C., Ryan, P., and Pavia, M. (2013). *Heating and cooling* [online]. Available at: https://www.yourhome.gov.au/energy/heating-and-cooling [Accessed 30 Jan. 2021].

18 Department of Industry, Science, Energy and Resources (2020). *Solar PV and batteries* [online]. Available at: https://www.energy.gov.au/households/solar-pv-and-batteries [Accessed 30 Jan. 2021].

19 Passipedia (2020). *What is a passive house?* [online]. Available at: https://passipedia.org/basics/what_is_a_passive_house [Accessed 29 Jan. 2021].

20 Ambrose, M., and Syme, M. (2015). *House Energy Efficiency Inspections Project*. CSIRO. Available at: https://research.csiro.au/energyrating/wp-content/uploads/sites/74/2016/05/House-Energy-Efficiency-Inspect-Proj.pdf [Accessed 30 Jan. 2021], p.10.

21 The University of Melbourne (2018). *Energy-efficient homes attract premium sale and rental prices, study finds* [online]. Available at: https://about.unimelb.edu.au/newsroom/news/2018/may/energy-efficient-homes-attract-premium-sale-and-rental-prices-study-finds [Accessed 30 Jan. 2021].

22 Wikipedia (2021). *Building airtightness* [online]. Available at: https://en.wikipedia.org/wiki/Building_airtightness [Accessed 30 Jan. 2021].

Chapter Ten

23 National Construction Code (2019), Volume 2, V2.6.2.3 [online]. Available at: https://ncc.abcb.gov.au/ncc-online/NCC [Accessed 30 Jan 2021].

24 Reardon, C. (2013). *Sealing your home* [online]. Available at: https://www.yourhome.gov.au/passive-design/sealing-your-home [Accessed 30 Jan. 2021].

25 Ambrose, M., and Syme, M. (2016). *Air tightness of new Australian residential buildings*. Available at: http://www.sbe16sydney.be.unsw.edu.au/Proceedings/31864.pdf [Accessed 30 Jan. 2021].

Chapter Eleven

26 Merriam-Webster. *Overcapitalize* [online]. Available at: https://www.merriam-webster.com/dictionary/overcapitalize [Accessed 30 Jan. 2021].

27 Feagins, L. (2019). *The Design Files' top 10 architectural homes of 2019*. [Online]. Available at: https://thedesignfiles.net/2019/12/architecture-best-architectural-homes-2019 [Accessed 30 Jan. 2021].

Chapter Thirteen

28 Farrel, B., and Farrel, P. (2016). *Men Are Like Waffles, Women Are Like Spaghetti.* Eugene, OR: Harvest House Publishers.

29 The University of Melbourne & ArchiTeam (2018). *Do small practice architect designed renovations improve capital gains in the Melbourne residential property market?* [online] Available at: https://www.architeam.net.au/static/uploads/files/rasp-final-report-wfknlfyqtpqy.pdf [Accessed 5 Feb. 2021], p.20–22.

Chapter Fourteen

30 Australian Institute of Health and Welfare (2020). *Home ownership and housing tenure* [online]. Available at: https://www.aihw.gov.au/reports/australias-welfare/home-ownership-and-housing-tenure [Accessed 30 Jan. 2021].

THANK YOU FOR READING MY BOOK!

I really appreciate your feedback and would love to hear about your Future Home journey!
Connect with me through **studiom514.com.au**

Please leave me an honest review on Amazon, letting me know what you have learnt from the book and which parts of the book were useful to you.

THANK YOU SO MUCH!
~FARINAH HUSODO~